THE REAL READER'S QUARTERLY

Slightly Foxed

'Making the Best of It'

NO.56 WINTER 2017

Editors Gail Pirkis & Hazel Wood

Marketing and publicity Stephanie Allen & Jennie Harrison Bunning

Bookshops Anna Kirk

Subscriptions Hattie Summers, Olivia Wilson & Katy Thomas

Cover illustration Clare Curtis, 'The Thought Fox', linocut

Clare has worked in print, design and illustration for over twenty years. The craft of drawing and printing are as important to her as the strong design, patterns and beautiful colour combinations that you'll find in her work. As a lover of print and plants in equal measure, she is increasingly exploring our relationship with plants and nature, and our nation's passion for gardening. A linocutter first and foremost, Clare uses traditional materials and methods to create her prints. Lino blocks are meticulously hand cut, each colour being printed separately to create a distinctive and beautiful original artwork. For more of her work visit www.clarecurtis.co.uk.

Design by Octavius Murray

Layout by Andrew Evans

Colophon and tailpiece by David Eccles

Published by Slightly Foxed Limited

53 Hoxton Square

London N1 6PB

tel 020 7033 0258

fax 0870 1991245

email office@foxedquarterly.com

www.foxedquarterly.com

Slightly Foxed is published quarterly in early March, June, September and December

Annual subscription rates (4 issues)
UK and Ireland £40; Overseas £48

Single copies of this issue can be bought for £11 (UK) or £12 (Overseas)

All back issues in printed form are also available

ISBN 978-1-910898-09-3

ISSN 1742-5794

Printed and bound by Smith Settle, Yeadon, West Yorkshire

Contents

Contents

John Watson

For the digital edition of *Slightly Foxed* and an up-to-date list of partners
and membership benefits, please visit the members' page on our website:
www.foxedquarterly.com/members or contact Olivia:
olivia@foxedquarterly.com · +44 (0) 20 7033 0258

The Slightly Foxed office can obtain all books reviewed in this issue,
whether new or second-hand. Please contact Anna:
anna@foxedquarterly.com · +44 (0) 20 7033 0258

From the Editors

From the start, we were keen that *Slightly Foxed* should feature not only contributors familiar from other book pages but also the voices of people who could write but who didn't think of themselves as writers – people outside the literary world, who had other equally interesting kinds of experience, and for whom the written word was just as important. We've come to the conclusion that this describes many of our readers, judging from your sparky entries to the writers' competitions we've run in the past. So, now the dark evenings have closed in again, we think it's a good time to run another one.

This year's competition is open to all *Slightly Foxed* subscribers and the winner will receive a prize of £250. We're looking for a piece of between 1,000 and 1,500 words on a favourite book (do check our online index to make sure it hasn't been covered already) or on a personal experience that is 'book-related'. You'll find more about the competition on our website, www.foxedquarterly.com: entries should reach us by 31 March 2018.

Meanwhile Christmas is almost upon us again. We receive so many cheering letters from people who have been given gift subscriptions and have then decided to go on and renew independently that we conclude it's a present that hits the spot for any bookish friend or relative. And there's much more tempting merchandise for the bookish in the enclosed winter catalogue – plus of course the whole range of Slightly Foxed and Plain Foxed Editions, a collection of voices and personal experiences so various that there's bound to be something to appeal to anyone who enjoys the art of memoir. At the end of the catalogue you'll also find our ninth literary crossword.

Entries should reach us no later than 14 January 2018 and the first correct one drawn out of a hat will receive a free annual subscription.

Our winter SFE this year is Erich Kästner's *When I Was a Little Boy* (see p.13), an account of growing up in Dresden before the First World War by the author of *Emil and the Detectives*. It's a charming book, delicate and humorous but shot through with a strain of melancholy as Kästner remembers his childhood in the 'wonderful city, full of art and history,' that was flattened by the Allies in 1945. In many ways those early years were idyllic – Erich's main problem was that both parents loved their only child to an almost suffocating degree. Yet, as so often, out of this intense and emotionally complicated childhood came a most unusual writer, who drew on it to create one of the best-loved children's books of the twentieth century.

On the subject of children's books, we have some hot news. In the spring we'll be adding a hitherto unpublished volume to Ronald Welch's Carey series. The manuscript of *The Road to Waterloo*, which follows the events leading up to that great battle, was recently re-discovered among his papers by his daughter. This new slim volume, which fills a small but significant gap in the Carey family story, will be hand-numbered and part of the limited edition. Copies can be pre-ordered now (UK £14; overseas £16 *inc. p&p*).

It's a strange new world we live in, isn't it? Among the many emails that arrive at the office we recently received one encouraging us to watch a video in which a journalist at 'News Republic' would tell us 'how their obsession with end-user experience delivers value for publishers'. Sorry? We looked up 'News Republic' and discovered that it 'leverages editorial, algorithmic and community intelligence to offer the widest possible perspective' on the news. And so, dear end-users, we hope we'll continue to deliver value to you during the coming year and offer you the widest possible perspective. Or as we used to say, we wish you all a peaceful Christmas and plenty of good reading in 2018.

GAIL PIRKIS & HAZEL WOOD

Making the Best of It

WILLIAM PALMER

'One day there appeared at luncheon sitting opposite to us a rosy, gray-bearded, bald-headed, gold-spectacled old gentleman who captivated my attention . . . Something seemed to bubble and sparkle in his talk and his eyes twinkled benignly.' This was one small American girl's first meeting with Edward Lear in 1870. At about the same time he was writing of himself in his diary: 'Broken down with a hideous load of sorrow – the blinding accumulation of now nearly 60 years.'

When Vivien Noakes's biography, *Edward Lear: The Life of a Wanderer*, was first published in 1968, the cartoonist Ronald Searle hailed it as 'magnificent . . . as constantly fascinating as Lear himself'. This was deserved praise for the woman who devoted herself to revealing the many talents of the man too often seen simply as runner-up to Lewis Carroll as the great Victorian children's writer. Her work continued. In 1985 she curated an important exhibition at the Royal Academy that was a revelation of the full range of Lear's achievement as a landscape artist, and in 1988 she edited both a selection of his extensive correspondence and *The Complete Nonsense and Other Verse* for Penguin Classics.

I never read Lear as a child and was only introduced to what he called his 'nonsense' when I read his poems to my daughter, then

Vivien Noakes, *Edward Lear: The Life of a Wanderer* (1968), is out of print but we can obtain second-hand copies.

aged 7. Now, thirty years later, I find myself reading them to my granddaughter, aged 5. The long poems, such as 'The Owl and the Pussy-cat' and 'The Dong with the Luminous Nose', continue to work their magic, though some of the limericks can be a little difficult to explain:

> There was a Young Lady in White,
> Who looked at the depths of the night:
>   But the birds of the air,
>   Filled her heart with despair,
> And oppressed that Young Lady in White.

This, like a lot of Lear, has a grown-up melancholy, and if you read it to a young child you may be met with an enquiring upward look, as if to say 'What's that all about?' But I think we underrate Lear's appeal to children and exaggerate that of Carroll. And as men? Well, Carroll's rather cold, Oxford bachelor-don personality is well known, but I had no idea of the mixture of warmth and terrible darkness in Lear's life until I read Vivien Noakes's book.

Edward Lear was born in 1812 in Holloway, London, the penultimate of twenty-one children. His father was a stockbroker, but even for a wealthy man such a huge family was a considerable burden, and when he got into financial difficulties the family was split up, with the older children having to find work and the younger ones being farmed out to relatives. Edward, then aged 4, was left in the charge of his 25-year-old sister Ann.

The difficulties of family life were horribly exacerbated two years later when he suffered the first attack of what he called 'the Demon' – epileptic fits that occurred almost every day, and sometimes several times a day, for the rest of his life. He quickly learned to recognize an oncoming attack, to hide himself away and to suffer each in complete isolation. It seems that no one outside the immediate family circle ever became aware of his condition or of the accompanying sense of loneliness and shame he called 'the Morbids'. It's not surprising that moments of happiness in his childhood stood out with great clarity:

> The earliest of all the morbidnesses . . . must have been some-
> where about 1819 – when my Father took me to a field near
> Highgate, where there was a rural performance of gymnastic
> clowns &c – and a band. The music was good . . . & the sunset
> & twilight I remember as if yesterday. And I can recollect cry-
> ing half the night after all the small gaiety broke up.

He did not go to school until he was 11 and the experience was painful. What saved him from complete despair was being taught by his sisters to paint and draw. His natural talent was such that he was able to support himself as a freelance artist from the age of 15.

His work was his salvation. Many years later he wrote, 'I HATE LIFE unless I WORK ALWAYS.' He started off ignominiously, selling sketches to coach passengers in the yards of inns, but he rapidly became a sought-after illustrator of natural history books. A folio of drawings of parrots, published before he was 20, was judged to equal if not excel the great Audubon and led to an invitation to the Earl of Derby's estate to draw the animals in a private menagerie. Initially regarded as a servant, Lear was found so amiable and entertaining that he was soon invited to dine with the family. In the next few years he was passed from one aristocratic family to another, each charmed by the large, ungainly young man who was an ideal guest, able to draw, sing, play the piano and flute and, above all, amuse their children with his verses and stories.

When Lord Derby and others clubbed together to provide him with enough money to go to Rome for two years, in return for drawings he would make for them, Lear found liberation in simply being away from England. A letter home explained, in his own idiosyncratic way, that 'The walking – sketching – exploring – noveltyperceiving & beautyappreciating part of the Landscape painter's life is undoubtedly to be envied – but the contrast of the moneytryingtoget, smoky dark London life – fuss – trouble is wholly odious and every year more so.'

The wanderer lived and worked in Italy, Greece, Corfu, Albania, Turkey, Egypt, Palestine and India. Breezily accepting the most difficult of living conditions and often travelling through virtually unexplored country, he worked from dawn to dusk at watercolours, drawings and the landscape oil paintings that he hoped to sell for large sums. He was mostly disappointed, but by unceasing activity he was able to make a reasonable living and to remain free. The number and radiant beauty of the works he produced on his travels are a triumph of spirit over private depression and suffering.

But it is for his 'nonsense' that most of us remember Lear. His first work for children, *A Book of Nonsense*, containing his limericks and extraordinary, grotesque drawings, appeared in 1846 and was followed by a book of verses, stories and comic alphabets. But the nonsense – if it was such – was not something concocted to charm children. It spilled out from his personality in the almost surreal verbal contortions and drawings that fill the letters he wrote to friends.

Like most of the great Victorians, Lear wrote letters almost every day. They confide some of his troubles candidly, but they are also full of the joy he found in new places and people. He always maintained that he was weak at drawing the human figure – but the cartoons of Lear himself, as a tall, heavy figure dancing, painting or walking in great strides on legs as long as stilts are a delight. It seems that he was alternately embarrassed and intrigued by his own appearance: he portrays himself with his arm around a huge and rather bashful parrot, astride a runaway elephant, accompanied by huge frogs, one on each arm, dressed as an archbishop, or disguised as a bespectacled and besuited owl or bee or snail. In many of the later drawings he is accompanied by his wily-looking cat, Foss. (Lear adored Foss – so much so that when forced to move from his house in Italy, he had an exact copy built so Foss would feel quite at home in new surroundings.)

One drawing in the letters that comes as a mild shock is of three young women in India dressed in what look like bikinis. Lear says 'they are the most virtuous of people', but goes on to tell his correspondent, Lord Carlingford, that as many of 'these worthy females are perfect in shape & very pretty . . . it might be well that you should make some public suggestion that so economical and picturesque an apparel may be brought into general use in England'.

Despite this lively appreciation of women, Lear never married. Vivien Noakes believed he was a suppressed homosexual, and he did indeed become very attached to the younger men who sometimes accompanied him on his travels. He invested deep trust and feeling in these relationships and was devastated when they ended, but we are too quick to regard all close friendships of the Victorian era as sexually driven. After all, Lear left plenty of evidence in his diaries and letters that he pined after marriage, and he came close on more than one occasion. But it seems that whenever he thought he might propose his nerve failed him. What he thought of as the hideous and shameful secret of his epilepsy would inevitably be revealed. This deeply affectionate man was also horribly sure that he was not a fit mate for anyone. In his final book of verses, published when he was in his sixties, he wrote with affecting sadness of his position:

> 'Lady Jingly! Lady Jingly!
> Sitting where the pumpkins blow,
> Will you come and be my wife?' –
> Said the Yonghy-Bonghy-Bò.

'I am tired of living singly, –
On this coast so wild and shingly, –
I'm a-weary of my life:
If you'll come and be my wife,
Quite serene would be my life!' –
Said the Yonghy-Bonghy-Bò.
Said the Yonghy-Bonghy-Bò.

There is a tolling valedictory sound in those last two lines that sums up what he told his diary: 'Accept a lonely destiny . . . & make the best of it.'

In later life Lear settled in San Remo, with Giorgio, his faithful Greek servant of many years, and Foss. He had taken to drinking large quantities of marsala as, unfortunately, had his servant, and the odd couple often fell to arguing. Lear also began to have trouble with his sight and attacks of dizziness. He continued to work but was now hardly able to sell anything at all. It was at this low point that he drew together his last and greatest verses in *Laughable Lyrics* (1877), including the wonderful 'Dong with a Luminous Nose', 'The Courtship of the Yonghy-Bonghy-Bò', 'The Pelican Chorus', 'The Quangle Wangle's Hat', 'The Pobble Who Has No Toes' and other poems whose combination of sadness and humour sum up his own life and which have provided pleasure and enchantment to others ever since.

Edward Lear, most brave and amiable of spirits, died in 1888.

WILLIAM PALMER's latest novel, *The Devil Is White*, was published in 2013. A collection of his poetry, *Endland*, was published by Rack Press in 2017.

48 Königsbrücker Strasse

SUE GEE

Erich Kästner was born in Dresden on a snow-
filled February day in 1899, the adored only
child of Emil and Ida Kästner: he a master saddler fallen on pinched
times, she – eventually – a hairdresser. Each had begun life in small-
town Saxony, Emil coming from a line of joiners and blacksmiths, Ida
with a background in bread, beer, butchery and horses. 'And out of all
the butchers, blacksmiths and horse dealers, one solitary member of
the family, little Erich, only son of little Ida, has become – of all things
– a writer!'

When I Was a Little Boy (1957) is the autobiography of this clever,
spirited, loving child, who grew up to write political journalism,
screenplays and children's books. His adult life in the Third Reich
was often difficult, even dangerous, but not a breath of that disturbs
these pages of affectionate recollection.

Writing in his fifties, Kästner looks back on the days of trams and
of parades before the Kaiser, with his huge moustaches. He recalls
doing homework by the light of a smoky paraffin lamp, and running
errands before school, returning to his third-floor family flat with a
spilling can of paraffin and a bulging bag of liver sausage, black
pudding and a huge warm loaf. There, he is given a slice with hot
malted coffee, before he grabs his home-made satchel and races off to
school. And though in adult life he travelled far from his birthplace,
his love for it shines through in almost every chapter.

First, there is Dresden itself, 'a wonderful city, full of art and
history', where 'past and present lived in perfect unity . . . and
harmonized with the landscape – the Elbe, the bridges, the slopes of

the surrounding hills, the woods, the mountains . . .' He loved the glittering shop windows at Christmas, and 'the vista of the city in silhouette, with its noble and venerable towers', but the cramped little flat at the shabby end of the Königsbrücker Strasse where he grew up was far from this ancient grandeur.

> I remember No. 48 perfectly well – the vestibule, the window-seat on which I used to sit looking down at the backyards, the steps of the stairs on which I used to play. For the staircase was my playground. It was here that I used to set up my fort . . . Fierce battles took place here . . . And the postman, and little Frau Wilke who lived on the fourth floor, had to take enormous steps, like storks on a bed of lettuce, in order not to endanger either the victory or the defeat.

Erich Kästner had the gift, which most clever children have, of concentrating completely on the task at hand. In this, perhaps, he was most like his quiet, undemanding father, who could make or mend anything well – a saddle, a bridle, a briefcase, a marvellous Christmas toy. But essentially, in that little flat, Erich was his mother's child, and all *her* concentration was on him.

Ida Augustin had grown up with brothers and sisters on an isolated farm, and one of the most appealing of the delightful illustrations in this book is of her determinedly making her way across a snowy field towards the distant school, leaving a long line of tiny footprints. She was clearly very bright, but the choice of career for such a girl in the late nineteenth century was limited: you went into service or you married. An introduction by her aunts led her to the sober, industrious young Emil Kästner, who was looking for a capable partner in life.

For Ida this meant dutiful cooking, bookkeeping and piece-work corset-making until, after seven years, the longed-for baby finally made his appearance. And with this little creature her drive, devotion and ambition finally found direction. 'All her love and imagination, all her industry, every moment of her time, her every thought – in fact her whole existence, she staked, like a frenzied gambler, on one single card – on me! . . . She loved me and nobody else', and at home and at school there seemed no option but for Erich to become the perfect son. 'I dared not disappoint her.'

Reading this with modern eyes, one might think that here was potential for disaster, but this model child flourished, and *When I Was a Little Boy* is largely filled with the everyday happiness of a close-knit, hardworking family. While her husband, after a day at a suitcase factory, earns extra money mending neighbours' bags and purses, Ida trains as a hairdresser, and a corner of their flat becomes her successful salon. At school, Erich is soon at the top of the class. He is athletic, and from the age of 5 determined to excel at gymnastics. He's also a responsible boy: when Ida's rich, horse-trading brother Franz buys a grand villa not far away, his wife Lina entrusts little Erich with the task of carrying large bags of money to the local bank. And he has good friends, with whom he plays in the summer holidays.

Through all this activity he has since earliest childhood one ambition: to become a teacher. This is fed partly by natural inclination and partly by the lodger his parents squeeze into the flat. Cheerful young Paul Schurig takes the 'beautiful sunny room with breakfast'; young Erich has plenty of opportunity to observe the teaching life: the routine, 'the blue exercise books and the corrections in red ink', the afternoon naps before the evening marking. His parents applaud his choice of career, but it takes just one lesson, when he stands before a class at the age of 17, for him to realize he has made a mistake. 'I was no teacher, I was a learner.' That evening he breaks the news to his parents: what he wants to do is go to university. It takes but a moment for his mother to declare, 'Very well, my boy. You shall study!'

When I Was a Little Boy won the international Hans Andersen

Medal in 1960, and it is a delightful book. The tone is gentle and avuncular, indefinably Germanic, filled with aphorisms and asides to the reader. Its optimism and buoyancy are shaded only occasionally by sadness. Of the city he so loved, bombed to pieces by the Allies in 1945, Kästner writes bleakly, 'It had taken centuries to create its incomparable beauty. A few hours sufficed to spirit it off the face of the earth.'

 Other sorrows lie closer to home. Though he generally loves his life as an only child, at Christmas Erich longs for brothers and sisters. To enter a room filled with presents – an elaborate toy stable, with exquisite tiny mangers filled with hay, made by his father; a heap of 'roller skates, building bricks, coloured pencils' from the shops of Dresden, bought over weeks by his mother – is to find the weight of their love for him almost unbearable. What will happen if he seems to like the gift of one parent more than that of the other? It is a huge relief when they can all leave and make their way through the snowy streets to his aunt and uncle and cousin Dora, for spiced buns, games and carols.

The other poignant passage relates to Ida's intermittent periods of depression. The illustrations by Horst Lemke are generally charming – light, spry, filled with sharp observation and humour. But all at once, you find yourself looking at something very different: a sky filled with black clouds, a tiny figure looking down from a bridge at the racing waters of the Elbe. Erich has returned from school to find a note: '*I can't go on.*' He bolts out of the door and makes for the river, shouting wildly, 'Mamma! Mamma!' And eventually he finds her, and she lets him bring her home.

'The last chapter did not sound very cheerful,' Kästner writes. 'A child was troubled, and that child was myself. Perhaps I should not have told you about it? No, that would have been wrong of me . . . he who denies that trouble exists would be a liar.'

And as he would gently say, troubles are made to be overcome: his mother does recover. In his adolescence they take long hiking trips together, a further opportunity for Kästner to indulge his love of *stuff.* The book is filled with lists: of saddlery tools, hairdressing equipment, school books; and here are the essentials for these summer days: 'iron-tipped alpenstocks, a Thermos flask, containers for butter, sausages, eggs, salt, sugar and pepper, a saucepan for heating Maggi soups . . .' The lists serve to anchor the narrative both in the period and in the author's sensibility: here is someone who makes the most of everything he finds in the world around him.

It is the First World War which brings his childhood and youth to a close. No one can yet imagine that Erich Kästner will become the author of one of the best-loved children's books of the twentieth century, in which the son of a hairdresser joins with new friends to track down a thief to a bank in Berlin. *Emil and the Detectives* (1929) has been translated into almost sixty languages. In 2013 my friend Carl Miller adapted it for the National Theatre's Christmas production, and it was seeing this brilliant piece of theatre which led me to Kästner's classic memoir.

SUE GEE is at work on a new novel, *The Summer of Für Elise.*

Erich Kästner's *When I Was a Little Boy* (216pp), illustrated by Horst Lemke and translated from the German by Isabel and Florence McHugh, is now available from Slightly Foxed in a new limited and numbered cloth-bound pocket edition of 2,000 copies (subscriber price: UK & Eire £16, overseas £18; non-subscriber price: UK & Eire £17.50, overseas £19.50). All prices include post and packing. Copies may be ordered by post (53 Hoxton Square, London N1 6PB), by phone (020 7033 0258) or via our website www.foxedquarterly.com

Introducing M. Swann

ANTHONY WELLS

This is the first of three articles on Proust's novel Remembrance of Things Past. *The second and third will follow in issues 57 and 58.*

The first time my wife-to-be invited me round for a meal, and sat me down in her book-lined dining-room, my eye was caught by three thick volumes in a slipcase, in decorative blue, white and red dust-wrappers, bearing the name 'Marcel Proust' in large black letters at the top of each spine. 'You've read Proust!' I burst out, thrilled to be able to add to the array of charms with which she had already dazzled me that of having read the incomparable *Remembrance of Things Past* (*À la recherche du temps perdu*).

'Well, yes and no,' she replied. 'Part of it. The first part, in fact, the one about Swann. For some reason, I didn't get any further.' Looking more closely, I noticed to the side of the three-volume set a paperback edition of the first of the novel's seven books, *Swann's Way*, so

---

The first translation of Proust's novel, the one I spotted on my wife's bookshelf, was by C. K. Scott Moncrieff, who had completed his version of the first six books by the time of his death in 1930. The final book – at that point entitled *Time Regained* – was translated by others. This edition is available from Vintage in six paperbacks. It is also available in hardback, in a four-volume boxed set, from Everyman at £65 (ISBN 9781857152500).

This original English version underwent further revisions before, in 2002, a new translation was commissioned by Penguin, this time not from one single person but by several hands. That edition is available from Penguin, also in six paperbacks. I have used both translations for the quotations in these articles.

well-thumbed it was nearly falling apart. 'You have a treat in store, then,' I said, 'reading the rest.' 'Yes, I must get round to that – when I have time,' she added, a note of hesitancy in her voice.

As it happened, an opportunity to read more arose not too long after this conversation. It turned out that my beloved suffered intermittently from insomnia. Normally, she would try to read herself back to sleep, with varying degrees of success. So, as an eager lover anxious to please, I suggested I read to her in the hope that this would lull her to sleep, as bedtime stories had in childhood. But what to read? We tried several writers, without success. One she found too exciting, another too childish, another – Henry James, if I remember rightly – too much of a syntactical puzzle to be restful. Then it occurred to me: how about Proust? We might be able to kill two birds with one stone, simultaneously combining the inducement of sleep with the completion of the remainder of Proust's great novel. Clearly it might take some time, since the more successful a soporific Proust proved, the longer we would need to reach the end. Still, it was surely worth a try.

The first time I read her Proust at night, his gently meandering sentences put her back to sleep by the end of the first paragraph. This success was amusing in its way, since we had agreed to begin again at the beginning, and the novel's opening pages are about falling asleep:

> For a long time, I used to go to bed early. Sometimes, when I put out my candle, my eyes would close so quickly that I had not even time to say to myself: 'I'm falling asleep.' And half an hour later the thought that it was time to go to sleep would awaken me; I would make as if to put away the book which I imagined was still in my hands, and blow out the light; I had gone on thinking, while I was asleep, about what I had just been reading, but these thoughts had taken a rather peculiar turn; it seemed to me that I myself was the immediate subject of my book . . .

From these first lines, the narrator goes on to tell us about the half-memories and phantasms that his half-conscious state conjures up, and the difficulty he has, waking in the dark, in identifying the objects in the surrounding gloom. He fails to recognize in which of the many bedrooms of his life he now finds himself. Gradually, in the uncertain light, the shapes resolve themselves into the familiar furniture of his present room – his chest of drawers, his writing-table, his fireplace – and he is now wide awake. His memory has been stirred

and, like my wife in her own sudden returns to wakefulness, he does not go back to sleep at once but spends much of the night recalling his past life, starting, appropriately enough, with bedtime in his childhood, at his great-aunt's house in the village of Combray, when his mother would come up to kiss him goodnight.

Marcel Proust (right) with his brother Robert

One kiss was never enough, he would want to call her back for another but feared that if he did so he would incur her displeasure, keen as she was to get him out of the habit of needing this goodnight kiss, of which his father so disapproved and which she feared would be the ruin of his character. But the evenings when his mother spent such a short time in his room were infinitely preferable to those

on which we had guests to dinner, and therefore she did not come at all. Our 'guests' were usually limited to M. Swann, who, apart from a few acquaintances, was almost the only person who came to our house at Combray, sometimes for a neighbourly dinner (more rarely after that unfortunate marriage of his, because my parents did not want to receive his wife), sometimes after dinner, unexpectedly.

It is in this way, just fourteen pages into the 3,000-plus page novel throughout which he will be such an influential and ubiquitous pres-

ence, that Charles Swann – the man who lends his curious surname
(for a Frenchman) to that first book of the novel *Swann's Way* or, in
a later translation, *The Way by Swann's* – makes his first entrance.

*

This first book of Marcel Proust's *Remembrance of Things Past* – or *In
Search of Lost Time* as it is now better known – appeared in 1913 and
the last in 1927, five years after its author's death. The span of time
the whole novel covers is close to fifty years, although it is difficult to
know exactly, since almost no dates are mentioned. It is a fictional
autobiography which recalls, broadly, the childhood, youth and
maturity of the narrator but, thanks to the character of Swann, also
extends to a period contemporaneous with the narrator's infancy and
earliest childhood, years containing events which he can only learn
about from others.

In Search of Lost Time is a single novel comprising within it seven
individual books. The first – using the titles of the most recent
English version – is *The Way by Swann's*, the second *In the Shadow of
Young Girls in Flower*, the third *The Guermantes Way*. Book four is
entitled *Sodom and Gomorrah*, books five and six *The Prisoner* and
The Fugitive respectively, and the seventh and final book *Finding
Time Again* (*Le Temps retrouvé* in the French original). There is a
chronological progression through the novel, but because the interest
of the novel is as much in the great cast of characters and the narrator's reflections on them (and on himself) as on the story, it seemed
to me more appropriate to organize these essays around the three
main protagonists and the themes they represent, rather than trace
the plot step by step through the seven books.

The years the novel portrays are those from the late 1870s to the
early 1920s, a time when – until 1914 at least – French society and
culture were so vibrant and inventive, and things French and Parisian
exerted such an attraction beyond France's borders, that periods
within it have come to be known by their French names – the *fin de
siècle* and the *Belle Époque*. (Some historians, when asked, have said

that this is the age and place in which they would have wished to be alive.) For this – the years of the Third Republic – was a time of innovation and change, when electricity began to replace gas, the horse-drawn carriage gave way to the motor-car, the railway network expanded (allowing the narrator to travel to the Normandy coast for holidays, and to Venice), when the first telephones arrived, Kodak cameras became widely available, moving film was invented and the first aeroplanes rose into the skies. Medicine and pharmacology, too, were developing: the first X-rays were taken, new drugs such as morphine and aspirin became available, and new medical ideas – psychosomatic illness for one – were in the air. (The narrator is very keen on the new terms *neurotic* and *neurasthenic*, which seem to fit his excessively nervous disposition like a glove.)

However, this brave new world of modern technology will belong more to the younger man, the narrator, than to the older figure of Charles Swann, the former's mentor, precursor, hero and – in some respects negative – role model. Swann may be a family friend of his solidly upper-middle-class parents (though their deprecation of his *demi-mondaine* wife has reduced the frequency of his visits to their house in Combray) but he belongs to a different world and moves in more elevated circles.

Swann is a member of the most select private gentleman's club in France, the Jockey Club, despite being a Jew. He is a personal friend and adviser of the Duchesse de Guermantes and her husband, the head of one of France's oldest aristocratic families. What he advises on is their purchase of art, since he is an art historian and connoisseur, as well as a prominent collector, lending – as the narrator's great-aunt reads in *Le Figaro* – one of his Corot paintings to an exhibition in Paris. A Rubens, we are told later, hangs above the fireplace of his Paris sitting-room.

Swann is also a friend of Elstir, one of the new school of Impressionist painters, and of the novelist Bergotte, whose writing the narrator is not alone in admiring so fervently. Swann helps form the boy's taste, recommending to his grandmother prints of Old Master paintings to give her grandson, inspiring in him an interest in the cathedrals and old churches of France, encouraging him to visit the Normandy coast to see the church of Balbec, and supporting his desire, opposed by his parents, to see the great actress Berma play her celebrated and eponymous role in Racine's *Phèdre* on stage.

It is also through Swann that two other great themes of the novel are introduced: love and sex. The first girl the narrator falls in love with is Swann's daughter, spied through a gap in the hawthorn hedge at Swann's country house near Combray; and the second object of his desire is the girl's mother, Swann's wife Odette, to whom the narrator transfers his adolescent longings after the daughter proves indifferent. To the narrator, Mme Swann is a glamorous figure of fashion, swathing herself in the latest dresses and fabrics, festooning her drawing-room with exotic cut flowers, garnering the tributes of the men-about-town who doff their hats to her as she takes her walks down the avenues of the Bois de Boulogne. Only later, when he enters the world of the salons, does he learn – from others – the reason why his parents refused to meet her and why they regarded Swann's marriage to her as 'unfortunate'.

What he then discovers reveals to the reader another aspect of French social life in the late nineteenth century, the world of the *demi-monde*, of kept women and mistresses, of licensed tarts and unlicensed streetwalkers, of *maisons closes* and *maisons de passe*, the brothels and 'houses of assignation'. This is the Paris of upmarket houses of pleasure such as the Chabanais, for which the Prince of Wales (mentioned in the novel as part of Swann's circle) designed his notorious love seat and which other princes and even crowned heads of Europe, and statesmen, diplomats, lawyers and wealthy business-men are said to have patronized so indefatigably.

According to historians, there were 235 licensed brothels in Paris in the 1890s and an estimated 35,000–40,000 prostitutes. It is to this world that Swann's mistress Odette belongs. In Odette, Proust has created an embodiment of the professional courtesan of the time: mercenary, manipulative, socially ambitious, using her erotic power and intuitive understanding of the weaknesses of naïve rich gentle-men to get them to support her and to shower her with jewels and other precious gifts. She grants just enough of her favours to keep them begging (Odette drives Swann almost mad with jealousy) before – if she's successful – finally inveigling them into marriage.

The story of Swann's love affair with Odette sets the pattern for the narrator's own tortured obsession later in the story with a girl he meets at the seaside resort of Balbec. The narrator's search for the psychological laws of love, revealed in both Swann's and his own affairs, runs parallel to his other searches – for lost time, for the laws of human sexual behaviour of all kinds, and for the laws of social change, exemplified in one way in the tale of the one-time *grande horizontale* Odette and, in another, by those members of the *gratin* – the absolute upper crust – of French society, the Guermantes. It is the Guermantes and their world – which, once she had been intro-duced to them, put an end for good to Proust's efficacy as a soporific for my wife – that will be our next subject.

ANTHONY WELLS has spent the best part of a lifetime avoiding putting pen to paper, prevaricating with a number of occupations including monitoring East German radio for the BBC, librarianship and running a family business. He hopes it's going to be a case of better late than never.

Secrets of the Hive

NICHOLAS ASPREY

In my school holidays, over fifty years ago, I used to cycle from our family home into Guildford to visit the second-hand bookshops. At the top of the High Street was the vast and wonderful emporium of Thomas Thorp, where the heavily laden bookshelves looked as though they might topple over in a cloud of dust at any minute. In Quarry Street, by contrast, was the magisterial bookshop of Charles Traylen who was described in his obituary in *The Times* as 'the last of a breed of grandees of the antiquarian book trade'. Situated in Castle House it was a place in which to browse and to dream, and it was here that I spent much of my time.

Our home was in the village of Worplesdon. It stood in an ancient garden where, as a member of the Home Guard, my father had performed lookout duty during the war from a crow's nest built high up in an oak tree and from which he could see for miles around. The owners at that time were three spinster sisters, each of them called Miss Thompson. My father bought the house from them in 1947. They were cousins of P. G. Wodehouse and he used to stay there with them before the war. No doubt this accounts for the character known as Lord Worplesdon who, it will be recalled, was the husband of Aunt Agatha and once chased a young Bertie Wooster 'a mile across difficult terrain with a hunting crop' for smoking one of his special cigars.

The Thompsons had performed their patriotic duty during the war by growing vegetables in the garden and my parents now set

Maurice Maeterlinck, *The Life of the Bee* (1901)
Dover · Pb · 176pp · £6.99 · ISBN 9780486451435

Miriam Macgregor, 'Somerset Garden', woodcut

about restoring it to its former glory. One of its main features was a pair of herbaceous borders separated by a lawn some six feet wide that was covered in white frost on cold mornings. It intrigued me that spiders were able during the night to spin their silky aerial skeins across the lawn from the delphiniums on one side to the phlox and hollyhocks on the other – a minimum distance of eight feet – without any intermediate support. It was probably this glimpse into the world of these miniature scaffolders that caused me on one of my visits to Traylen's bookshop to fasten on a copy of Maurice Maeterlinck's *The Life of the Bee*, translated from the French by Alfred Sutro and published by George Allen in 1901. I snapped it up for ten shillings, took it home on my bike, began to read and was transported.

Bees have fascinated mankind since earliest times, as evidenced by rock paintings across Africa and elsewhere. The bibliography of bees goes back a long way too and Maeterlinck provides a brief survey from Aristotle and Pliny down to his own day. Real scientific study began in the seventeenth century with the discoveries of the Dutch savant Jan Swammerdam who dissected bees under a microscope and finally settled the sex of the queen, 'hitherto looked upon as a king'; and by the end of the nineteenth century great strides had been made in the practice of beekeeping by the invention of movable and artificial wax combs and the honey extractor.

However *The Life of the Bee* is not a scientific study or a treatise on practical beekeeping but a study of the bees and their culture written by a man who had observed them during twenty years of beekeeping. 'The reader of this book', he says, 'will not gather therefrom how to manage a hive; but he will know more or less all that can with any certainty be known of the curious, profound and intimate side of its inhabitants'; and he writes 'as one speaks of a subject one knows and loves to those who know it not'. Each episode in the life of the hive is described, including the laws, the habits, the peculiarities and the events that produce and accompany it: the formation and departure of the swarm; the foundation of the new hive; the birth, combat and nuptial flight of the young queens; the massacre of the males; and the return of the sleep of winter.

Maeterlinck is not content to rest there. What he sets out to do is explain *why* they behave as they do: that is, with extravagant care for the hive and each other on the one hand and yet with savage cruelty and recklessness on the other. He seeks to identify a unifying principle that explains why, for example, they offer the queen loving care and protection while she is laying her eggs but then cynically abandon her when she has ceased to be fertile; or why they tolerate the presence in the hive of several hundred males – those 'foolish, clumsy, useless, noisy creatures, who are pretentious, gluttonous, dirty, coarse, totally and scandalously idle, insatiable, and enormous' – only one of whom will be chosen to impregnate the new queen, and then, at the appropriate time, 'coldly decree the simultaneous and general massacre' of every one of them.

Fundamental to their behaviour is what he calls 'the essential trait in the nature of the bee': namely, that it is a creature of the crowd. When the bee leaves the hive to go foraging it behoves it, under pain of death, to return at regular intervals 'and breathe the crowd as the swimmer must return and breathe the air'. If it does not, and however abundant the food or favourable the temperature, it will die within a few days. From the hive it derives an 'invisible aliment' that is as necessary to it as honey. This craving, he says, helps to explain 'the almost perfect but pitiless society' of the hive where 'the individual is entirely merged in the republic' and the republic in turn is invariably sacrificed 'to the abstract and immortal city of the future'.

This spirit of the hive explains all the behaviour of bees, he concludes, including the allocation of work among them. It allots their respective tasks to

the nurses who tend the nymphs and the larvae, the ladies of honour who wait on the queen, and never allow her out of their sight; the house-bees who air, refresh or heat the hive by fanning their wings, and hasten the evaporation of the honey that may be too highly charged with water; the architects, masons, waxworkers and sculptors who form the chain and construct the combs; the foragers who sally forth to the flowers in search of the nectar that turns into honey, of the pollen that feeds the nymphs and the larvae, the propolis that welds and strengthens the buildings of the city, or the water and salt required by the youth of the nation.

Skilfully, almost as if telling a story, Maeterlinck unravels the secrets of the hive and transmits his fascination and curiosity to the reader. Each chapter is broken down into short sections and this reduces a complex subject to simplicity and clarity. It is not merely a pleasure to read; in places it is gripping. He was, of course, a skilled writer and in 1911 was awarded the Nobel Prize for Literature 'in appreciation of his many-sided literary activities'. It is not surprising, therefore, that he is able to rise to the occasion. His description of the nuptial flight, for example, is almost as breathtaking for the reader as for the virgin queen and her tragic consort:

> She rises still. A region must be found unhaunted by birds, that else might profane the mystery. She rises still; and already the ill-assorted troop below are dwindling and falling asunder. The feeble, infirm, the aged, unwelcome, ill fed, who have flown from inactive or impoverished cities – these renounce the pursuit and disappear in the void. Only a small, indefatigable cluster remain, suspended in infinite opal. She summons her wings for one final effort; and now the chosen of incomprehensible forces has reached her, has seized her, and, bounding aloft with united impetus, the ascending spiral of their intertwined flight whirls for one second in the hostile madness of love.

Maeterlinck carried out numerous experiments with bees and made notes of his observations. He is credited by modern science with being the first to discover that bees communicate with one another. Scientists have now shown *how* they communicate, namely by a series of dance steps. He also suggested that the survival of the human race might depend on the survival of the bees, and scientists have now endorsed this view. Anyone wishing to read more deeply into the subject can do so by referring to such works as M. L. Winston's *Biology of the Bee* (1987); but for the ordinary reader *The Life of the Bee* provides a perfect introduction. It is a little gem.

NICHOLAS ASPREY has now retired after 45 years in practice at the Chancery Bar and has taken up writing articles on subjects of interest to him. He is a Governing Bencher of the Inner Temple and a member of the Library Committee and has served as Editor of the Inner Temple Yearbook.

Aerobatics

MATT HUBER

Gavin Lyall was not the first pilot to take to fiction – Nevil Shute, Ernest K. Gann and Antoine de Saint-Exupéry navigated the skies creatively before him – but Lyall's thrillers of the 1960s and '70s set a standard of aerial pace and style that has not been bettered. When his first novel, *The Wrong Side of the Sky*, was published in 1961 P. G. Wodehouse was prompted to write: 'Terrific! When better novels of suspense than this are written, lead me to them.'

The novel set a pattern Lyall was to follow in three further thrillers, all featuring the seat-of-the-pants adventures of pilots for hire: *The Most Dangerous Game* in 1964, *Shooting Script* in 1966 and *Judas Country* a decade later, in 1975. His third novel chronologically, *Midnight Plus One*, published in 1965, features a car chase through France rather than a pilot, but it could just as well be classified in the flying genre since Lyall treated driving the car, the iconic 1950s French Citroën DS, much as he did flying an aircraft.

Common to all Lyall's flying thrillers are the narrators. Though they may differ in name, they have in common a dry laconic wit and throwaway lines of the kind pioneered by Dashiell Hammett and Raymond Chandler. All are experienced fliers of battered integrity, seen-it-all cynics who are tough under pressure and have hearts, if not of gold, then at least in the right place. One identifies with them

---

Gavin Lyall's aviation thrillers – *The Wrong Side of the Sky* (1961), *The Most Dangerous Game* (1964), *Shooting Script* (1966) and *Judas Country* (1975) – are all out of print but we can obtain second-hand copies. *Midnight Plus One* (1965) is available as an Orion paperback (304pp · £8.99 · ISBN 9780752867175).

and, thanks to Lyall's powers of description, one is with them up there in the cockpit – of a Dakota, the wartime and post-war work-horse of the skies, in *The Wrong Side of the Sky*; a Beaver amphibious float plane in *The Most Dangerous Game*; a de Havilland Dove and a worn-out US wartime Mitchell bomber in *Shooting Script*; and a Beechcraft Queen Air in *Judas Country*.

Gavin Lyall knew about aeroplanes because he'd both flown them and covered aviation as a journalist. Born in 1932, he served as a pilot in the RAF before going to Cambridge where he edited *Varsity*, the university newspaper. As a journalist, he worked for *Picture Post* and the *Sunday Graphic* and later became air correspondent of the *Sunday Times*. In this latter role he wrote an early profile of the Anglo-French Concorde, still under construction, opening his report in typical Lyall style: 'Concorde has always been a bit of a bastard. When it was officially conceived in . . . 1962, its parents, Britain and France, were not married – although as usual in such matters, one partner expected they soon would be.'

I was introduced to Lyall's novels by a friend much taken, as I was to be, by the author's often sardonic style – 'Pushing fifty and not moving it much', 'A few years younger than me and about a century younger than I felt', or, on entering a hotel bar, 'I'd forgotten the lighting they went in for there: a small frosted-glass lamp parked in front of each drinker. Just enough light to make every woman look beautiful and every bar bill unreadable. A big hotel thinks of such things.'

In tune with the times in which they were written and set, and like films of the post-war period, Lyall's stories feature characters who smoke and drink heavily, whether in the air or on the ground. The cockpit floor of one plane becomes its ashtray; a bottle of beer from a sympathetic engineer in the maintenance hangar is de rigueur for a typical Lyall pilot with a hangover landing his plane. It is devil-may-care buccaneering of the highest order, and the rust-bucket planes are as battered as their pilots. The Beaver in *The Most Dangerous Game* is described thus: 'one of the floats was slightly out of line, the fuselage was twisted so that none of the doors fitted properly, and the engine bearings were waggling like a film star's bottom'.

Lyall undertook much research for his books, travelling widely and ensuring that scenes and locations live on the page. *The Wrong Side of the Sky* is set in the Greek Aegean islands and Libya, well before Colonel Qaddafi. The plot, like those of several of Lyall's early thrillers, involves a hunt for stolen treasure and features gun fights, carousing and pretty, usually intelligent and headstrong women. His next novel, *The Most Dangerous Game*, is about long-lost treasure, the search for valuable minerals via aerial survey, murder, mayhem and espionage, all set within the Arctic Circle. The 'most dangerous game' of the title is Man himself when armed with a gun – and the ending is not pretty.

Improbable though they all may be, what nevertheless lifts each plot is Lyall's ability to carry the reader with him. One is in the hands of a writer skilled in describing exactly what it is like to fly a plane, often in extreme weather conditions. Here is an Italian Piaggio private plane heading into a Mediterranean storm:

> [Ahead rose] a rampart of great white thunderheads reaching to 40,000 feet . . . eight-mile high pillars of thunder stuffed with roaring up-and-down currents that could flip a 100-ton jetliner on her back and then tear the wings off her. To a little four-tonner like the Piaggio it would be like flying through a meat mincer . . .
>
> For a moment [the plane] was still, passive . . . Then the vertical currents hit us. The Piaggio reared on a wing-tip, fell off before I could catch her. Then we surged upwards, hung and dropped. There was no point in fighting her . . .

In *Shooting Script*, Lyall's cynical Jamaica-based British charter pilot takes on flying for a film company in the

From the dust jacket of *Shooting Script*

Caribbean. His passengers include a Hollywood actor in the John Wayne mould and the plot itself is very Hollywood, but the story also features one of the author's very best descriptions of an aircraft – the wartime B25 Mitchell bomber mentioned earlier. The plane has not been used for years. Then its next pilot-to-be enters the cockpit for the first time:

> I took a slow, deep breath. The Mitchell smelled. Of petrol and oil and hydraulic fluid and plastic and leather and sweat, but all adding up to some new, strange smell that would be the way all Mitchells smelled . . . I took a high step forward and . . . eased into the left-hand pilot's seat, being careful not to touch any lever that might drop the whole plane on its backside. No switch should, of course, but who repairs safety locks after twenty years?

Somewhat improbably, the Mitchell is then used in a Caribbean coup, dropping not bombs but house bricks on an aerodrome, a scenario that Lyall manages to make plausible.

Gavin Lyall went on to write about espionage, both contemporary and set in the early years of the British secret service – in the 1980s *The Conduct of Major Maxim*, starring Charles Dance, was filmed for television. These novels enjoyed commercial and literary success, and Lyall twice won Crime Writers' Association awards. Yet in the opinion of his wife, the renowned *Observer* writer Katharine Whitehorn, he was, in creative terms, the victim of bad luck or at least unfortunate timing. In her autobiography *Selective Memory*, she tells of the actor Steve McQueen wanting to play a lead character in *Midnight Plus One* and MGM buying the option – only for McQueen to die before the film could be made. Then, when *Judas Country*, the last of Lyall's flying thrillers, set in Cyprus, came out, the Turkish invasion of the north of the island effectively dated the story immediately.

Gavin Lyall himself was tall and imposing and gracious. When I once met him and enthused about his aviation stories, he said he did not feel he could keep them going endlessly – in particular because, in order to write credibly, he needed to get to know and fly the aircraft featured in each novel. Hence his later move to another genre.

Bookshops these days tend to segregate fiction, consigning 'thrillers' and 'crime' to their own sections away from mainstream novels. But, as writers like Gavin Lyall demonstrate, an adventure-thriller can be every bit as creative in its evocation of a place or an activity as supposedly more 'serious' novels. Second-hand bookshops, such as remain, tend to be less compartmentalized. This is where the aviation novels of Gavin Lyall are likely to be found – for those readers ready to fasten their seat belts and take to the skies in the hands of a skilled and entertaining pilot-author.

MATT HUBER's first flight was in an old Dakota. Ever a nervous passenger, he prefers reading to flying.

A Writer in Hiding

KATE JONES

I first saw A. L. Barker's books lined up in a row on a shelf in the University of East Anglia library, their dust covers removed, their red, blue and green cloth bindings faded, their pages clean and unmarked – it seemed as if they'd never been read. I borrowed the books and read them one after another. Here was a writer who clearly deserved attention. Her fiction seemed so contemporary, not in terms of style but because of the ideas with which it grappled: the strangeness of so-called ordinary life; the dangers of ignorance or innocence; the consequences of taking, and not taking, action.

I wanted to know more about her but there was little information available – a few obituaries, a couple of mentions in academic monographs. The bare facts were these. Audrey Lilian Barker was born in 1918 at St Paul's Cray in Kent and grew up in Beckenham. She left school at 16 because her father, a railway worker, didn't believe in further education. During the war she served as a Land Girl and married. The marriage was not a success and she later said that it failed because she was selfish: for her, writing was the main thing. She worked for the BBC for three decades, including five years as a sub-editor on *The Listener*. After the war she lived with a friend, Dorothy McClelland, and achieved the domestic stability that she needed to write. In all she wrote nine short-story collections (including ghost stories) and eleven novels, published over a period of fifty years. She died aged 83 in Sutton, Surrey, only sixteen miles from her birthplace.

A. L. Barker, *Innocents* (1947), *The Joy-Ride and After* (1963), *The Middling* (1967), and *Life Stories* (1981) are all available as Faber Finds, priced at £13 each.

In the late 1930s A. L. Barker worked with an all-male team of girls' fiction writers in the department of juvenile fiction at the Amalgamated Press. The experience is hilariously described by Barker in her autobiography and short-story collection, *Life Stories* (1981). The time she spent writing the adventures of idealized child figures with names like 'Sally-Never-Grow-Up' influenced her subsequent lifelong interest in writing stories about children for adults, a fine example being her first short-story collection, *Innocents* (1947), which won the inaugural Somerset Maugham Award and allowed her to travel in France and Italy.

Speaking about 'The Art of Fiction' in the *Paris Review* in 1981, Rebecca West said of Barker: 'She really tells you what people do, the extraordinary things that people think, how extraordinary circumstances are, and how unexpected the effect of various incidents . . . The people come off the page to tell you what this would be like. You feel: Now I understand this better.'

High praise indeed, though Barker must have been surprised as well as delighted by West's account of her as a writer focused on the extraordinary and unexpected. In *Life Stories*, she insisted that she had no desire to write about the events in her 'predictable' life; readers, she felt, 'were accustomed and entitled to lives that were rich and/or strange'. Much to her dismay, however, she *did* want to write about how the events in her life had affected her writing. Her anxiety about doing so stemmed from the idea of 'all those pages, x-hundreds, it could be x-thousands, peppered with I's'. Bearing in mind that by this point Barker was in her early sixties, a Fellow of the Royal Society of Literature, a member of PEN and the author of a novel that had been shortlisted for the Booker Prize, her reticence is surprising.

For Barker, though, privacy was key. Her inhibition about revealing herself on paper started at an early age. In *Life Stories* she writes: 'When, for the first time, something I had written appeared in print I hid it. Seeing my thoughts on a page was humiliating. One of two

courses was open to me: I should have to destroy whatever I wrote, or I should have to write like someone else. I wanted nothing of myself on paper.' In the short stories, especially, Barker experiments with writing 'like someone else'; but, of course, she could not avoid putting herself on paper – and much of her best writing is clearly marked by a profound dissatisfaction with that self.

In *The Middling* (1967), for instance, as Ellie Toms waits in her ill-fitting school uniform to collect third prize in the County Literary Festival Essay Competition, she sees herself through the eyes of the usher: 'I looked like a number three, third-prize material, well down the scale, at the bottom, in fact, of this particular one because there were no Consolation Certificates. I hated him and everyone there . . .' Ellie's sense of being third-rate, both socially and intellectually, is echoed in Barker's description in *Life Stories* of her secondary schooling at a girls' grammar school: 'I felt mandatory, the pip put in to show that the jam was made with real fruit.' And later, in a statement tinged with her customary wry humour: 'I had got a scholarship on a mistaken estimate of my abilities . . . I was at that school, that stronghold of knowledge and wisdom and the future, under false pretences. The Authorities had been grossly deceived. When I left . . . I imagined them saying: "We won't be caught like that again."'

Social class played an important role in Barker's sense of herself as an interloper. Her background was unusual considering her profession; female working-class writers were rare in the 1940s and 1950s. In *Life Stories* she lists the staff at the house where her mother worked: 'a nurse, a cook, a house-maid and a gardener, and my mother to do the rough cleaning'. As well as reminding the reader of the still-rigid hierarchy of British society in the early 1920s, Barker emphasizes her parents', and her own, place within it. But unlike her mother and aunts, who 'all had self-sufficiency and were happy about themselves',

Barker's awareness of her social class – and her adolescent attempts to distance herself from it – resulted in feelings of estrangement from both school and home.

Navigating literary London was clearly a trial for a young working-class woman with such a sense of intellectual and social inferiority. In the spring of 1948, soon after the success of *Innocents*, Barker attended a party at the West London home of John Carter, the manager of Scribner's London rare book business, and his wife, the journalist Ernestine Carter. Barker was taken ill at the party, and afterwards was haunted by the idea that perhaps Ernestine and John thought she had been drunk: she had to be reassured by her editor and friend, Norah Smallwood of the Hogarth Press.

Such an acute concern for how people perceived her must have played a part in her position on the margins of the literary scene. Avoiding social events in London, she preferred to remain at home in Carshalton Beeches. Of course there were also practical and financial reasons for her absence from the city: she worked full-time in various secretarial and assistant roles, which were not well paid and left little spare money, time or energy for socializing. One can't help but wonder, though, how Barker saw herself in the eyes of people like Ernestine Carter. Most of the literary people she knew were from upper- or middle-class backgrounds. Perhaps she felt about the literary scene the way she felt about her grammar school – the pip put in to show that the jam was real.

Barker's writing, like her writing life, is characterized by a tension between revealing and concealing. Although the short story was her preferred form, the finest examinations of secrecy and self-censure are in her novels. In *The Joy-Ride and After* (1963), for example, Alice Oram's role as a housewife and mother in middle-class suburbia constrains her when she discovers that her husband is having an affair:

> She ached for violence, to beat out the other woman like dust out of a carpet. She wanted to strip the place clean of Lilly Warren,

her hands yearned to start. She thrust them under her armpits and the energy ran up her arms and exploded inside her head.

She fell back on words. They came off her tongue, breathy at first, then like a flock of dirty birds – words decent women find they know when put to it. It was some relief to utter them until they started dropping back – slut and harlot and whore came plumping all round her. In the thick of it she caught sight of her daughter.

Alice's subsequent switch back into her role of the 'decent woman' and ideal mother doesn't fool her teenage daughter, Grace. Committing thoughts to words transforms the private into the public, uncovering a secret self that, once revealed, cannot be pushed back under the surface.

Barker's fiction reflects her awareness of the irreversibility of self-exposure. Her writing checks itself and keeps aloof, cautious about revealing too much. There is a quietness to her work that is often mistaken for conservatism, a lack of energy, or disengagement from social and political concerns. In a review of *A Source of Embarrassment* in the *Financial Times* in 1974, Isabel Quigly wrote of 'the almost impenetrable inner world of A. L. Barker' and noted her 'quiet reputation for sharpness, precision, perfect finish'. Reviewing the same novel in the *Observer*, Anthony Thwaite described Barker as a 'delicate, muted novelist' who 'writes in a witty undertone, stylish, oblique, with a sense of claws beneath the surface . . . like a 1970s Jane Austen'.

Barker always considered herself to be a 'spare-time writer' and her fiction to be somehow different or apart from that of other highly regarded writers. In her archive in the Harry Ransom Center at the University of Texas, Austin, I found what appears to be her response to a list of questions about her writing from an academic researcher: 'V. S. Pritchett, Walter de la Mare, Katherine Mansfield, Elizabeth Bowen, Daphne du Maurier – and a host of others classic and modern

– I admire and envy *because they demonstrate how it should be done.*' The words in italics replace the original phrase, 'but cannot think they have influenced my work', which was crossed out. Barker's reluctance to admit the influence of other writers on her work is yet another example of her underestimation of her talent. She feels that these writers 'demonstrate how it should be done', suggesting that her own writing falls well below this ideal standard. I disagree with Barker about the merit of her work and hope that, over time, others will not only appreciate her writing but also recognize her importance. As Norah Smallwood put it in a letter to Barker in 1951: 'For a distinguished Prize winner your modesty is unequalled. And never have I met a more self-critical writer . . . But that's why you're so good.'

Like Smallwood, I admire Barker because she wrote despite a sense of inadequacy, harnessing the pernicious voice of self-criticism rather than allowing it to silence her. She is a writer who kept aloof – but kept going. She wrote through her own and others' doubts about her writing, during all those years of commuting from Surrey to poorly paid jobs in London. Barker is a writer for all those readers, writers and thinkers who feel uncertain, insignificant or overlooked, who are haunted by the spectre of an ideal standard and how things 'should be done', but who keep on reading, writing, thinking and talking about books regardless, and eventually find their audience.

KATE JONES's Ph.D. thesis was on A. L. Barker's work and writing life. She now teaches at the University of East Anglia and lives in Cambridge with her partner, her son, her cat and her books.

Sixty Years On

MICHAEL BARBER

Back in the days when I used to read to my son at bedtime I was very struck by something Janet Adam Smith said in her introduction to *The Faber Book of Children's Verse*. You will find, she said, that poems you learn when you're young remain with you far longer than those you learn later. So in addition to 'giving pleasure now', she hoped her collection would 'stock up the attics of your mind with enjoyment for the future'.

Oddly enough it was thanks to my wife's discovery recently in a real attic that I was able to test Miss Adam Smith's theory. Nestling in a box full of bric-à-brac was her father's copy of *The Dragon Book of Verse*, a book I had last opened about sixty years ago at my prep-school, where it was used for a weekly exercise called 'Rep'. He had bought it second-hand for 2/6d during the year he spent at Oxford before being called up. Before that it had belonged to a boy at St Edward's, Oxford, who had coloured in many of the quaint illustrations.

For some of you the *Dragon Book* will need no introduction. It is as redolent of the classroom as *Kennedy's Latin Primer*, Marten and Carter's history books and, on a lighter note, *1066 and All That* and *Down with Skool!* But I wonder how many people could name the *Dragon Book*'s editors? They were both called Wilkinson, as indeed

---

The Dragon Book of Verse celebrated here and published in 1935 by the Clarendon Press is out of print but copies are available second-hand. In 1977 Michael Harrison and Christopher Stuart-Clark produced a new edition for OUP, which was followed by a third edition in 2000.

was the Worcester College don whose 'valuable assistance' they acknowledge in the Preface. So presumably they were all related? Well, no. Nor were the two editors lifelong colleagues. For while W. A. C. Wilkinson – always known as 'Wilkie' – spent thirty-four years at the Dragon prep-school, Noel Wilkinson taught there for only four years, leaving in 1935, the year the *Dragon Book* appeared.

What the Wilkinsons shared was a love of poetry and the urge to pass it on to their pupils in an unusually enlightened manner. Learning poetry, they believed, 'should be a delight and not a dreary task'. So rather than forcing a form to learn long poems 'week by week, verse by verse', they suggested that 'more often than not' pupils should be allowed to choose for themselves which poems to learn. I'm pretty sure this wasn't the case at my school, but I was one of the lucky ones for whom memorizing a poem – or an irregular verb – was not a struggle.

Understanding what one learnt was more of a challenge. But the Wilkinsons argued, correctly I think, that young people don't have to understand a poem to appreciate its beauty. Take 'The Owl Song' from *Love's Labour's Lost* – as earthy, it now seems to me, as a peasant painting by Bruegel. Even then it struck a chord that was not diminished by my failure to register that 'keel' – as in 'When greasy Joan doth keel the pot' – did not mean scour, but stir. In fact it wasn't until I reopened the book and read the editors' explanatory footnote that I realized my mistake.

'No book I have ever owned has given me more pleasure or, I believe, more profit,' wrote the poet and academic Jon Stallworthy, an Old Dragon himself, of this anthology. To him it was 'a period piece revealing of British middle-class attitudes between the wars'. Well, eighty plus years ago I suppose it was still just possible to believe that God was an Englishman. The Empire, lest we forget, was by then even larger than it had been under Queen Victoria. But I wonder if the presence of so many martial poems – 'Horatius', 'Lepanto', 'The Revenge' – was less a reflection of the 'imperial aspirations' Stallworthy identifies than of their harmony, the interplay of rhythm and metre that makes you want to read them aloud. Is there a more rousing opening to a poem than Chesterton gives 'Lepanto'? – 'White founts falling in the courts of the sun/And the Soldan of Byzantium is smiling as they run'. Closely followed by the first two lines of Byron's 'The Destruction of Sennacherib': 'The Assyrian came down like the wolf on the fold/And his cohorts were gleaming in purple and gold'.

That said, my early immersion in poetry that *sang* left me deaf to the appeal of what Edmund Wilson called 'shredded prose', his term for what was written by modern poets who had given up on verse. I know I should try reading it aloud, but I can't be bothered to make the effort. And whatever its merits, it can't be as easy to learn as lines that rhyme and scan.

Jon Stallworthy also notes that it took him a while to realize how many poems in the anthology offered lessons in dying. One such was Rupert Brooke's 'The Soldier', particularly cherished by my headmaster, like Brooke (and Stallworthy) an Old Rugbeian: 'If I should die, think only this of me:/That there's some corner of a foreign field/That is forever England . . .' Many years later, when writing a radio series on Appeasement, I learned that in the Thirties irreverent schoolboys gave a pert response to Brooke's exhortation: 'He did, and we don't.' Such cheek would not, I'm sure, have gone unpunished at the time by the editors; but based in Oxford they must have been aware that many of the Auden generation (as it had yet to be dubbed) were deaf to the appeal of King and Country.

Could this explain why they include only three poems by Kipling – then, I believe, more popular in Nazi Germany than in Great Britain – and nothing by Newbolt, the plucky public schoolboy's laureate? Housman is another notable omission. Perhaps he was considered too pagan. And yet what could be more pagan than this? – 'Golden lads and girls all must/As chimney-sweepers, come to dust'. Or this? – 'Sceptre and Crown/Must tumble down/And in the dust be equal made/With the poor crooked scythe and spade'. Or this? – 'The paths of glory lead but to the grave'. The writing was on the wall, all right, but aged 13 with your life before you, you could be forgiven for ignoring it.

HENRY V AT THE SIEGE OF HARFLEUR

O NCE more unto the breach, dear friends, once more;
Or close the wall up with our English dead!

There are no prizes for guessing that Shakespeare, with thirty-four, has the highest number of entries. For this I am especially grateful because I've not seen many of his plays and if I can quote snatches of his verse and recognize a whole lot more, it's thanks to the *Dragon Book.* How strange to think that I once won a prize for declaiming Hamlet's soliloquy and was soundly beaten for calling one of the assistant masters a 'lean and slipper'd pantaloon'. Another master, hearing me exaggerate my exploits on the rugger field, said I was far too young to start remembering 'with advantages', a caution I tried, with some success, to heed.

Browning, whose 'The Lost Leader' every political correspondent I've ever read seems obliged to invoke at least once, is well represented, and so too is Tennyson, who I'd forgotten wrote 'The Brook' ('I come from haunts of coot and hern'). Like my scapegrace contemporary,

Nigel Molesworth, the 'curse of st custards', I've never been able to remember the third line of this, echoing his version: 'and-er-hem-er-hem-the fern'. Molesworth, for whom 'peotry [*sic*] is sissy stuff that rhymes', gives qualified approval to 'The Charge of the Light Brigade', unaccountably missing here. I thought 'Jerusalem' was missing too, only to find it listed as *Part of the Preface to Milton*, the prosaic title Blake gave it, which was certainly news to me.

I must also admit how chastening it's been to encounter so many lines derivation of which I appear to have forgotten – if indeed I registered them in the first place. Take, for instance, the 'sneer of cold command'. What a wonderful expression, I thought, when I came across it in an essay. Was it in quotes? Maybe not. But even if it was I couldn't have told you that it came from 'Ozymandias'. Again, if you'd asked me who wrote, 'But westward, look, the land is bright!' I'd have answered Churchill, whereas in fact it was Arthur Hugh Clough. On the other hand we were certainly not encouraged to speculate about this line from Ovid's *Amores* that Marlowe gives to Dr Faustus: '*O lente, lente currite, noctis equi.*' In those days we didn't receive official notice of the facts of life until our last day at school, so to learn that this was the poet praying for time to stand still so he could spend longer in bed with his mistress would have let the cat out of the bag.

Had the Wilkinsons heard of Auden, then teaching at a Quaker prep-school near Malvern? Already hailed by Eliot as 'one of the four or five living poets worth quarrelling about', he was probably a little too outré to be included. And yet there was nothing outré about Auden's theories on poetry and the young. 'Do not enlarge on its beauties, but see that the vocabulary is understood . . . They will learn more about the meaning of poetry by writing it, than by any explanation you can give.' Many years later, when interviewed by the *Paris Review*, he said, 'If I had to teach poetry, I would concentrate on prosody, rhetoric, philology and learning poems by heart.' By then, rote learning, as its detractors termed it, was regarded as oppressive. Now we're told it's okay again, given the seal of approval by Salman Rushdie at last year's Hay Festival. He called it a 'lost art' that enriches your relationship with language – 'as any fule kno', I am tempted to add.

How much of what I learned as a boy have I retained? Well, rather more than anything I've tried to learn since, so Janet Adam Smith was right. But not as much as I'd have hoped, though of course it all comes back to me as soon as I look at the page, as is also the case with *The Book of Common Prayer*, another schoolroom text that was recited more often than read. From both I learned to appreciate, unconsciously but abidingly, the beauty of our native tongue.

Asked to choose a favourite when I was young I'm sure it would have been something stirring like 'Once more unto the breach' or 'Horatius'. Sixty years on I have lived longer than most of the poets in the anthology and, as the shadows start to lengthen, it is the elegiac that takes my fancy. Whether by accident or design there are, on the same page, two Shakespearian speeches that fit the bill: Macbeth's meditation on the death of Lady Macbeth and Prospero's 'Valediction'. I heard the last recently at the memorial service for a great man and it took my breath away.

MICHAEL BARBER would like to thank Gay Sturt, the Dragon School's archivist, for her help with this article.

No Coward Soul

CHRISTOPHER RUSH

Emily Brontë is the greatest woman novelist of all time. That is my personal opinion, though it is one which happens to be shared by many others, including highly respected scholars. That in itself is a compelling reason for reading the one and only novel she ever completed. How far her second novel had progressed will never be known, for her sister Charlotte, who often took it upon herself to act for her sisters in the way she thought fit, probably destroyed the manuscript after Emily's death.

Emily was born 200 years ago, in 1818. *Wuthering Heights* was published under the pseudonym of Ellis Bell nearly thirty years after her birth, in December 1847. It immediately excited some admiration for its originality, passion and power, but it also unleashed a barrage of abuse for its apparent brutality, its obsession with violence and vice, its immorality, savagery and disregard for civilized society. 'Coarse and loathsome' was the verdict of one critic. Another highly regarded man of letters, ironically admired by Charlotte, took it a step further: 'Coarse even for men, coarse in language and coarse in conception.' Though he could not have known it at the time, the irony was that Ellis Bell, who had written a novel too coarse even for men to read, was in fact the 29-year-old spinster daughter of a Yorkshire parson. Her life was circumscribed by religion, reading, the moors and the domestic routines of a remote parsonage in which she'd never have heard a coarse word, unless latterly from her drunken,

Emily Brontë, *Wuthering Heights* (1847)
Penguin · Hb · 354pp · £12.99 · ISBN 9780141040356

drug-addicted and doomed brother Branwell, whose misery and dereliction may have contributed something to one or more of the male characters in the novel.

And so on it went throughout the year. Emily Brontë as Ellis Bell was dubbed 'a spendthrift of malice and profanity', and her great creation, Heathcliff, as the 'epitome of brutality'. By the end of the year Emily was dead, dying at 30 of consumption (her coffin the narrowest the sexton said he had ever made), having expressed half amusement, half contempt for the sour abuse. She knew what she had written. She had flouted the conventions of polite writing and had to be punished.

At the same time many of those who disliked what they felt to be cruel and degrading also felt for it a horrified fascination: they were spellbound by its Ancient Mariner-ish power which revolted them but held them in thrall. They could not choose but hear; they could not choose but read on. The reviewer in Douglas Jerrold's *Weekly Newspaper* put it in a nutshell, admitting that while it confounded all regular criticism, 'yet it is impossible to begin and not finish it; and quite as impossible to lay it aside afterwards and say nothing about it . . . We strongly recommend all our readers who love novelty to get this story, for we can promise them that they never have read anything like it before.'

Not all the newspaper's readers followed the reviewer's recommendation. At least one husband and father cancelled his subscription to the paper forthwith and urged all decent husbands, fathers and brothers to do the same, spluttering his outrage that a hitherto respectable weekly should be encouraging and assisting the letting loose upon respectable households of such an obscene and disreputable book, which might even, perish the thought, be picked up and read by unsuspecting wives and daughters – or even servants.

For what my own personal recommendation is worth, I should say that by the time I picked up *Wuthering Heights* from the school library in my late teens, I had already read a great many of the classic eighteenth- and nineteenth-century novelists, including the women writers, of whom only Jane Austen bored me, as she did Charlotte Brontë, who famously lamented the suffocating atmosphere of her books, the absence of fresh air, wildness, vigour. So I had many points of comparison among novelists. But nothing, not even Mary Shelley's *Frankenstein*, could have prepared me for the profound effect which Emily Brontë's book had on me.

I was about as far from a parson's spinster daughter as any red-blooded male teenager could possibly get, and yet there were certain affinities. I was born and bred in a small rustic community. It was not as remote as Haworth but levels of mobility in the 1940s and 1950s were low, and the radius of my known world was three miles at most in any direction. I roamed the sea-shores as Emily did the moors. My sailor father was a Yorkshireman whose people occasionally visited our sea-girt village on Scotland's east coast, and years later when I first encountered the sternly repressive Joseph of the novel, my Yorkshire relatives leapt from the page in all their homespun glory. The coarseness, regretted by the reviewers, was a breath of fresh air, the fresh air Charlotte missed in *Pride and Prejudice*. And the moors of the book mirrored the sea of my peregrinations: both big and elemental, both constant but moody, both dwarfing the human infusoria under the microscope of the writer's watchful dissecting eye. I wasn't a writer yet, except in embryo, but my first books would be about how ordinary lives appear extraordinary when dramatized against larger landscapes, and against the inner landscapes of ritual and religion, superstition and dreams, storytelling and tradition, love and death. And of course grand passions.

Just about everybody who hasn't actually read *Wuthering Heights* has some vague idea at least that it is a novel dominated by the grand passion that exists between Catherine Earnshaw and Heathcliff, an affair that is not only endlessly unconsummated and deferred, but is ultimately inimical, destroying both lovers – if 'lovers' can even be specified as the correct term to describe a relationship that is unique in literature, and which transcends the idea of love as it exists in the romantic novel.

In a romantic novel they would have married, satisfying critical taste, but Catherine chooses instead the rather spiritless gentleman of the Grange, Edgar Linton, in spite of having admitted to Nelly the housekeeper that the choice is wrong. She does so in pages of impassioned prose, ending with the most famous declaration of devotion in literature, certainly in the history of the novel: 'Nelly, I *am* Heathcliff.' You have to go to John Donne to find anything approaching such a statement of oneness, of the union of souls. But Heathcliff does not hear this conclusion of her testimony, only her earlier avowal, that it would degrade her to marry him, at which point he leaves the house and disappears. When he returns three years later she is married, and moderately content – until that return cracks open the tragedy, and all hell is let loose.

Famously the story is opened years later in 1801 by Lockwood, Heathcliff's wealthy new tenant at Thrushcross Grange, and one of the novel's principal narrators. When he arrives at Wuthering Heights to introduce himself to his landlord, it is clear that all has yet to be revealed to him: he knows nothing of preceding events, or of much else beyond his own sheltered existence. He is blind, insensitive, inaccurate, complacent, shallow and a slave to convention, the last person you could imagine being disturbed by terrifying dreams. And this is where Emily Brontë's genius comes in, evoking a truly awful scene out of the mind of this unremarkable man, when a snow shower turns into a blizzard and he has to stay the night on the heights, an unwelcome guest. Moreover the servant puts him up in a forbidden upper room, with vague hints about happenings. Names have been scratched into the ancient paintwork of the window-ledge next to his bed: Catherine Earnshaw, Catherine Linton, Catherine Heathcliff. The mildewed library contains books in which Catherine's diary entries have been scribbled. The gothic clichés pile up. As he falls asleep the room swarms with Catherines 'as vivid as spectres'. He dreams and wakes up to the realization that amid the blizzard a fir-tree branch, driven by the wind, is rattling its dry cones against the panes of the lattice, working its way into the fabric of his dream.

Again he falls asleep and dreams a second time, only to be disturbed again by the tapping at the window. He sits up to put a stop to it, knocking his knuckles through the glass and reaching out to grab the offending branch – instead of which he finds himself clutching the fingers of a little ice-cold hand. It is the hand of Catherine Linton, sobbing to be let in. Terror turns the effete Lockwood cruel, and as he can't shake her off he saws the child's wrist across the broken pane until the blood runs down and soaks the bedclothes. Still he can't escape but he promises to let the ghost-child in if she will let him go. She does, and he breaks his promise by withdrawing his arm and blocking up the broken pane with books. But he can't shut out the lament, and her terrible wailing cry that she has been trying to get back into this room for twenty years.

Now Lockwood's shrieks of fear bring Heathcliff to the door of the forbidden room, no longer the grimly impassive landlord but a man visibly upset, shaken to the core by Lockwood's description of his vision. Lockwood is ordered to leave the room but in the darkness gets lost in the lobbies and so witnesses Heathcliff's next extraordinary action. He kneels on the bed, wrenches open the lattice and bursts into tears, sobbing for his Cathy, his heart's darling, to hear him *this* time, to come in at last.

Lockwood can't comprehend this raving, or the raw anguish in the gush of grief which accompanies it. After all only the snow and wind whirled through the open window, and that is all that was ever there. Any rational person could see it – there was no ghost. It was all a dream.

Or was it? It was that chilling scene, only three chapters into the novel, which made me see that Emily Brontë was opening a window on to a world in which dreams may overturn reality, the other world may break into our notions of normality, and heroic figures such as

Heathcliff may crumble helplessly before a helpless child. Later Lockwood becomes interested in the gossip, the history of Heathcliff and the house on the heights, but right now he doesn't want to know what happens next.

If you do, dear reader – want to know what happens next – then I am not about to spoil the story for you. But you will read a complex and brave and subversive novel, which explodes many of our safe assumptions – about the difference between men and women, heaven and hell, good and evil, love and hate, forgiveness and revenge, marriage and freedom, and about human identity and its survival. People used to ask, and some still do: how did the unmarried daughter of a country parson, with no experience of male relationships, come to write the most powerful love story in the world? Frustration, sublimation, empathy? Where is Emily Brontë in this novel? You might as well ask how Shakespeare, who never killed a king or strangled his wife, knew what it felt like to be Macbeth or Othello. Genius is the answer we have to be content with, the same answer and the only answer to understanding a phenomenon such as Bach or Mozart. They did it over and over again, and some would argue that it's in the repetition that the genius exists. But death has a way of foiling that simple test. And if you've already written one of the world's greatest novels, then even death has failed to rob you of your reputation. It may even enshrine it.

CHRISTOPHER RUSH has been writing for thirty-five years. His books include the memoirs *To Travel Hopefully* and *Hellfire and Herring*, and *Will*, a novel about Shakespeare. His latest novel, *Penelope's Web*, was published in 2015.

Packing a Punch

MORAG MACINNES

Pictures came before words. And as soon as there were pictures, there were funny pictures. I've always felt sanguine about the future of funny pictures, partly because they're also up-to-the-minute social comment, available to all, whether you're literate or not, in a war zone or a suburb.

My dad's painting studio had a bookcase along one wall, and I was allowed – if I was quiet – to look at the big books on the bottom shelf while he was painting his seascapes. Leonardo da Vinci was there, and Michelangelo, and Bruegel, and a Victorian book on drawing from the nude complete with fig leaves. But my favourite was a volume covered – as we used to cover our school books – in brown wrapping paper to protect the jacket. The wrapping paper was from the upmarket Edinburgh department store Jenners – or at least the Sellotape securing it was. This made me think it wasn't my Orcadian dad who painstakingly drew the title and the author on the front in red and green ink – PUNCH Pictures by REYNOLDS. He'd never have shopped there. Perhaps it was from a book sale.

Inside – a treasury, for a child who loved drawing and was just beginning to decipher and enjoy words. Picture after picture. Ladies with brollies. Golfers. Urchins. Soldiers. Buses and perambulators and train carriages and tea tables. All in scratchy, energetic, cross-hatched, left-handed pen and ink. I had my favourites before I even understood the jokes – a scared little man leaping a fence, a small boy in a chair surrounded by the film characters he was dreaming about, a fat lady in high heels with a fox fur eating itself round her neck.

Now I know far more about the illustrious history of *Punch* – but it wasn't till I took the book down last week to enjoy the drawings that I started wondering about the artist. Francis Reynolds, known as Frank, was born in 1876, an artist's son. Like me, he spent time in long and absorbed contemplation of his father at work and he loved messing about with the paraphernalia of the studio – the brushes, their heads wrapped in cotton, palette knives, baby watercolour boxes, nibs and mucky, crunchy charcoal. This boy also loved soldiers. He would walk miles to Piccadilly just to look in the window of a shop which sold military watercolours. Uniforms – their florid absurdity – absorbed him. He went into business, but it didn't work, and he became an art student at the forward-thinking Heatherley School of Fine Art, which allowed women to sketch nude men and emphasized the importance of structured drawing – something Frank took to heart.

He started his career drawing for the *Pick Me Up*, a satirical sheet in a blue wrapper. He frequented Belgravia and Bethnal Green with a notepad and pencil. He had a 'long stay' with two other cartoonists in France, stalking military types whose costumes were more colourful, and feathery, than their English counterparts, until he had all the details committed to paper. He sat for hours in open carriages, so that he could get the exact posture, beam width and hat dimension of the French cabbie in front of him. He – of course – visited Montmartre, especially a café called Le Lapin Agile, where there were beautiful downtrodden women and sleazy men to draw. Back in London at the music hall his gift got him into trouble. He made a cartoon of 'The Equilibrist' balancing cigar boxes and wine glasses on his toes and a lighted lamp on his head; an aggrieved Equilibrist threatened to sue because he was the only man in England who did that trick and Reynolds made it look too easy.

All the time he was trying to decide what his medium of choice really was. He did fine illustrations for Dickens – they're fluid and lively. He was elected to the Royal Institute of Painters in Watercolour in 1903. But the money was in cartoons; the middle class liked to laugh (within reason) at themselves, and loved to chuckle at those below and above them. Reynolds knew their world, and he loved absurdity.

Probably he was also having to make some decisions not unfamiliar to cartoonists now, in our *Charlie Hebdo* world. In 1913 he sent a couple of political cartoons to *The Leprecaun*, an Irish paper, right in the middle of the Dublin lock-out, ridiculing the police and mocking trades unionists. This foray into bitter politics was rare, however.

When war broke out, the owner of *Punch*, Sir Owen Seaman, thought seriously about putting up the shutters. Famously, he met a friend on the Tube and said, 'So, my job is ended.' 'On the contrary,' the friend replied, 'it has only just begun.' The War Propaganda Bureau held secret meetings with writers – H. G. Wells, Arnold Bennett, Conan Doyle, Hardy – and with the editors of *Punch*, to co-ordinate a patriotic approach. Cartoonists had never been so vital. There were reprints in popular papers of the 'Big Cuts' – the full-page political cartoons. Slide shows featured them as did postcards, cigarette cards, biscuit tins, vases, soap adverts. Most popular, initially, were those encouraging recruitment. Most popular of all – Frank Reynolds's 'Study of a Prussian household having its morning hate'.

I loved this cartoon long before I learned its context. There's a heavily curtained – I'm betting chenille – window with an aggressive pot plant. There's one of those hefty glass and brass lights you still find in Black Forest B&Bs. The picture frames are three times the size of the pictures. The upholstery is straining to escape its confines. The beer mug shouts pewter lid and serious decorative attention. The dachshund (Reynolds is very good at dogs) has the look of a hard Brexiteer.

And that's before we even get to the family gathered around the fringed tablecloth. Opa is apoplectic – he's stamping the newspaper into the ground. Oma is bursting out of her (comprehensive) corsets. Mutti is a spasm of disgust. Best of all are the children. The adolescent girl is lanky and malevolent; the small boy has a petted lip, puny clenched fists and buttoned shoes. It's perfect observation. It also encapsulates a very British feeling – that mild, county-cricket sense

of disbelief at the whole bally thing. 'Whatever did we do', this cartoon says, 'to make them hate us so much?' The *Daily Mail* reporter
in France wrote that the artist 'would feel his labours were amply
responded to if he knew how much his clever satire was appreciated
at GHQ in France'. It has reverberations now. Whatever have we
done to make them hate us so much, might well be a cartoonist's
battle-cry post-Referendum. Satire never loses its bite.

Of course, as the war progressed the cartoons became more subtle
and subversive. Reynolds stayed on the warmer side of criticism – he
was no Gerald Scarfe. In 1920, after fourteen years of drawing for it,
he became Art Editor of *Punch*, taking over from his brother-in-law.
Ten years later he had a nervous breakdown and stopped drawing for
a few years. I don't know why; but I have observed that cartooning –
and now, graphic novels – are a refuge for those who find the world
so impossibly harsh that the only way through it is humour. His
Second World War cartoons are a treasure trove of social observation.
A Scotsman sees a headscarfed, wellie-booted Land Girl passing by.
'Wumman, ye look terrible!' he says. (Alas, his Scots are all mean and
old-fashioned – but cartoonists don't do political correctness . . .) A
sergeant, barely of shaving age, addresses his elderly troop: 'Now lads,

I want you to look on me as a father . . .' A well-meaning lady hands out cigarettes to departing troops: 'Do try, these are home-made and herbal.'

Frank Reynolds died in 1953, but his work lives on, a testament to a world of Britishness which has perhaps departed, a world where the wife says to a grumpy little husband, across the dinner table – 'Did you not like the soup? Or did you have a bad golf round again?' As I leaf through the big book, I can't help but salute the craftsmanship. The drawing is just excellent. More than that though. You feel you're spending time with a very nice gentleman who had an eye for the idiotic absurdities of the British. Look out for his work; you'll like it.

MORAG MACINNES is an Orcadian writer.

"Look, Mummy! This is one they teach us!"

17 June 1942 © *Punch* magazine

An Extraordinary Ordinary Bloke

BRANDON ROBSHAW

What would you say if someone who knew nothing of George Orwell, beyond his name, were to ask you to recommend one of his books?

You might suggest *Animal Farm*. It's his most famous work: a witty satire on the Russian Revolution but with much wider application, written in Orwell's distinctive plain, vivid style, full of active verbs and concrete nouns. A pleasure to read though it undoubtedly is, however, it's a slight work – modestly described by Orwell himself as a fairy story, it is barely 30,000 words long and does not exhibit the full range of his talent or ideas.

Or you might say *Nineteen Eighty-four*. His last novel is a brilliant dystopian vision of a totalitarian Britain, drawing on the dictatorships of mid-twentieth-century Europe as well as Orwell's contemporary experience of post-war austerity Britain; it's bleak, it's grim and it's bitterly funny. It bestowed two new phrases upon the English language – 'Room 101' and 'Big Brother' (both of which became the titles of television programmes: can any other writer rival that?). Yet one feels it is not fully developed *as a novel*: the characters, except for the protagonist Winston, are lightly sketched in, and it's as much a vehicle for ideas as it is a work of art.

We can rule out his earlier novels. They are all very well worth reading; but they are all flawed in various ways. No, the book we should direct our enquirer towards is a collection of George Orwell's

George Orwell, *Essays* (ed. Bernard Crick, 2000)

Penguin · Pb · 496pp · £14.99 · ISBN 9780141183060

essays. That is where the reader will discover the quintessential Orwell. Bernard Crick, who edited the definitive Penguin collection, makes the point neatly in his introduction: giving the essays top billing clears up the puzzlement of those 'who believe that Orwell is a great figure but cannot honestly say that any one of his books measures up to his fame'.

The Orwell of the essays has a pungent literary personality. He's dauntingly knowledgeable, decided in his views and trenchant in their expression, a non-sufferer of fools, an enemy of pretension and hypocrisy; yet withal humane, reasonable, *decent.* He writes as if he's just an ordinary bloke – yet not an *ordinary* ordinary bloke, but an exceptionally well-read, politically aware, sensitive and intelligent ordinary bloke with wide-ranging interests and a view on everything. Just skimming through the titles of his essays gives one a sense of his range: 'Shooting an Elephant', 'Poetry and the Microphone', 'Anti-Semitism in Britain', 'Some Thoughts on the Common Toad', 'Good Bad Books', 'In Defence of P. G. Wodehouse', 'The Decline of the English Murder'.

Some of the essays are unabashedly highbrow; he's at his ease writing about James Joyce, or T. S. Eliot, or Salvador Dalí, or reviewing the latest book by Bertrand Russell. At the same time he loves to delve into the stuff of everyday life and report on its social, cultural or political significance: there are essays on seaside postcards, on boys' comics, on music-hall comedy. It has subsequently become common practice to subject everyday activities and events to intellectual analysis: semioticians do it, cultural studies dons do it, brainy journalists with English degrees do it. But it was Orwell who began the trend and to this day no one does it quite as searchingly, as wittily and as readably as he did it.

For Orwell, writing was never far removed from life. He brings the same energy, the same physicality to his prose as he would to making a table or digging a garden. One can recognize Orwell from a single sentence; his style is as distinctive as a hallmark:

[T]he toad, unlike the skylark or the primrose, has never had
much of a boost from poets.

All art is propaganda.

The human body is beautiful: it is also repulsive and ridiculous, a fact which can be verified at any swimming pool.

I grew up in an atmosphere of militarism, and afterwards I
spent five boring years within the sound of bugles.

Well-meaning, over-civilized men, in dark suits and black
felt hats, with neatly-rolled umbrellas crooked over the left
forearm, were imposing their constipated view of life on Malaya
and Nigeria, Mombasa and Mandalay.

Orwell set out his own views on prose style in his famous essay
'Politics and the English Language', written in 1946. He begins with
one of his trademark sweeping (but convincing) generalizations:
'Most people who bother with the matter at all would admit that the
English language is in a bad way, but it is generally assumed that we
cannot by conscious action do anything about it.' He then offers five
samples of recently published, cringe-inducingly bad English prose,
which amply bear out his contention that 'prose consists less and less
of *words* chosen for the sake of their meaning, and more of *phrases*
tacked together like the sections of a prefabricated hen-house'.

Bad writing of this kind has its attractions, as Orwell points out.
It is easier; the phrases are already there, at one's elbow. Moreover
they allow one to shroud ugly ideas in drifts of verbiage. Orwell
imagines

some comfortable English professor defending Russian totali-
tarianism. He cannot say outright 'I believe in killing off your
opponents when you can get good results by so doing.' Probably,
therefore, he will say something like this: 'While freely conced-
ing that the Soviet regime exhibits certain features which the
humanitarian may be inclined to deplore, we must, I think,
agree that a certain curtailment of the right to political opposi-

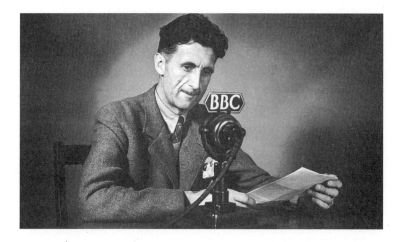

tion is an unavoidable concomitant of transitional periods, and that the rigours that the Russian people have been called upon to undergo have been amply justified in the sphere of concrete achievement.'

The connection between prose and politics is made clear: puffed-up prose allows one to defend the indefensible by means of euphemism, obfuscation and clichés that glide by without attracting notice. Toeing a party line is always bad for one's writing; it's only the rebels, the independent thinkers, whose writing is alive. Thus Orwell's call for clarity is political as well as aesthetic. But how to ditch bad habits and start writing prose that really does express an individual's thoughts, rather than pre-established positions? Orwell offers six rules:

i. Never use a metaphor, simile or other figure of speech which you are used to seeing in print.
ii. Never use a long word where a short one will do.
iii. If it is possible to cut a word out, always cut it out.
iv. Never use the passive where you can use the active.
v. Never use a foreign word, a scientific word or a jargon

word if you can think of an everyday English equivalent.
vi.   Break any of these rules rather than say anything outright
      barbarous.

Every writer should have those rules on their desk or desktop.

Prose was Orwell's natural medium. In his literary criticism his
comments on poetry are both astute and appreciative; but his own
attempts at poetry are slightly embarrassing. With prose he is playing
at home. For Orwell, prose is *the* vehicle of free thought and enquiry,
and the defining art form of what he calls 'the Protestant centuries'.
Orwell was an atheist, but he located himself within the individualist
tradition of Protestantism. In his essay 'Inside the Whale', referring
to the religious divide in Europe in the seventeenth century, he says:
'looking back, most modern people would feel that the bourgeois-
Puritan viewpoint was a better approximation to truth than the
Catholic-feudal one'. Not that this prevented him from admiring
certain Catholic writers. His point is that good writing does not tend
to emerge from uniformity of view; you can only write successfully
about what you believe in, not what you feel you *should* believe in.
All his essays in their various ways are a protest against bowing to
authority – or against 'the smelly little orthodoxies which are now
contending for our souls', as he put it.

The Orwell of the essays is rooted in Englishness. His world view
is informed by a deep love of his country, its customs and manners,
its history, its literature (he writes perceptively about the great English
writers, Shakespeare, Milton, Dickens), its scenery and wildlife. This
is not to accuse him of insularity. Far from it; he was internationalist
in outlook, and his life and work are more closely associated with
foreign lands than many other writers': Burma, where he served in
the Military Police for several years, out of which came his first novel,
Burmese Days; the Paris of *Down and Out in Paris and London*; the
Spain of *Homage to Catalonia*. Orwell's experiences abroad gave him
points of comparison the better to understand the country of

his birth: he begins his analysis of England in the extended essay 'The Lion and the Unicorn' by saying that English civilization is 'as individual as that of Spain'. The passages that follow have become justly famous for their lyrical evocation of an Englishness that comprehends 'solid breakfasts and gloomy Sundays, smoky towns and winding roads, green fields and red pillar-boxes'.

The essay is now over seventy years old, yet much of the English character Orwell described is still recognizable – our anti-intellectualism, our love of flowers, our fondness for hobbies and love of privacy, our bawdiness and love of drinking, our unarmed police and hatred of militarism, our hypocrisy and respect for the law. John Major quoted from this essay in a speech in the '90s (that bit about old maids biking to Holy Communion through the mists of an autumn morning) and it swiftly became the best-known speech Major ever made.

No doubt Orwell and Major would have disagreed politically about many things, but they have in common a love of their country. Orwell makes the point in more than one of his essays that patriotism tends to be sneered at by the Left. That's as true and as regrettable today as it was when he was writing. One can love one's country without being aggressive towards other countries; and one can love one's country yet see its faults and want to reform them. Orwell himself is proof of this.

One more aspect of Orwell's essays deserves comment, and that is his sense of humour. Perhaps Orwell isn't typically thought of as a funny writer, but he is. His combination of irony, indignation and brutal bluntness always brings a smile to my face. His essay 'The Sporting Spirit', written in 1945 after a British tour by the Moscow Dynamo football team, exemplifies these qualities. The only possible effect of such a visit, he says, would be to make Anglo-Soviet relations slightly worse than before. 'Even the newspapers', he says, 'have been unable to conceal the fact that at least two of the four matches played led to much bad feeling.' (I love the cynicism of 'Even the newspapers'

– as though it can be taken for granted that the usual business of newspapers is to conceal facts.) Serious sport, Orwell says, has nothing whatsoever to do with fair play: rather, it is 'bound up with hatred, jealousy, boastfulness, disregard of all rules and sadistic pleasure in witnessing violence'. This is a one-sided, exaggerated view but it's argued with such brio one finds oneself nodding in appreciation, especially when it comes to Orwell's brilliant peroration:

> If you wanted to add to the vast fund of ill-will existing in the world at this moment, you could hardly do it better than by a series of football matches between Jews and Arabs, Germans and Czechs, Indians and British, Russians and Poles, and Italians and Yugoslavs, each match to be watched by a mixed audience of 100,000 spectators.

Most journalism is by its nature ephemeral; but Orwell's essays leap off the page a lifetime after they were written. The Penguin edition runs to 496 pages: a considerable body of work, especially when one reflects that he was only 46 when he died.

Orwell believed in objective truth and hated pretension, double-standards and injustice. It's tempting to speculate about what he would have made of today's media, of the postmodernist grip on the humanities, of cultural relativism, of 'post-truth' politics. Fortunately, we still have his essays.

BRANDON ROBSHAW lectures in Creative Writing and Literature for the Open University. His 'young adult' novel, *The Infinite Powers of Adam Gowers*, is published by Unbound.

Well-Salted

YSENDA MAXTONE GRAHAM

Did we all have someone in our childhood who was The Best Giver of Presents? In my case, it was a family friend called Vere Guilford. She entered deeply enough into the person you were to get presents right. At the perfect moment she gave me a lockable cassette box. When my soul was starting to ache she gave me a double-cassette pack of Beethoven symphonies. At Christmas 1974 (I remember the mild disappointment on unwrapping it) she gave me Volume I of the twelve-volume *Oxford Junior Encyclopedia*.

It was the 'Mankind' volume of the 1974 edition, 500 pages long. With not much excitement I started to browse through this great red tome. It turned out to be more of a pleasure to browse through than the *Encylopedia Britannica* with its extensive articles on every single Pope – 'articles that tell you', as my father said, '*more* than you want to know'.

The instant appeal of this 'Mankind' volume was that it had photographs on almost every page to accompany the prose: large black-and-white ones of varieties of human I really wanted to look at, such as a family of pygmies smoking outside their hut. I spent the rest of Christmas Day gazing at such specimens: 'A gypsy family near Wexford, Ireland', 'A group of Bedouin', 'Hottentot women and children playing a game'. Accompanying the article on 'Races and Peoples' was a full page of photographs of faces: top row, 'Nordic, Alpine, Mediterranean'; middle row, 'Negro, Mongol, American

Some individual volumes of the *Oxford Junior Encyclopedia* (1974 edition), edited by Laura E. Salt & Geoffrey M. Boumphrey, are still available second-hand.

Indian'; bottom row, 'Melanesian, Polynesian, Australian Aborigine'. The faces got wilder and the hair more unkempt the further down the page you went. I don't think you'd be allowed nowadays to put the photos in that order. It implied some kind of hierarchy.

The following Christmas the same friend gave me Volume V: 'Great Lives'. Now I started lapping up the prose. No article is longer than 2,000 words; many are shorter, but none is pathetically short. The entries kick off with the person's greatness in a nutshell: 'Faraday was the discoverer of electrical induction, and therefore of man's power to generate electricity', but then they take you back to his or her child-hood. 'When he was five years old the Faradays moved to rooms over a coach house near Manchester Square in London; here at the age of ten Michael became an errand boy at a bookseller's shop . . .'

That was exactly the kind of thing a young person wanted to know, to humanize the man – and that volume has been indispens-able ever since for both my and my children's history and science projects. (Wikipedia articles are useless for such projects as they tell you *far* more than you want to know, and you don't even know whether you can trust them.)

From then on, I collected the twelve-volume set. The 'Law and Society' volume took over from 'Mankind' as my favourite as it con-tained fascinating illustrations and photographs of people having a horrible time: children playing football at a bleak borstal; a slave market in West Virginia; prisoners at a treadmill; men breaking stones in a workhouse; and the Metropolitan Police arresting two sus-pects after a theft at a department store. The last (and least-desired) volume to be acquired was Volume VII, 'Farming and Fisheries'. That one contained (under 'F') articles on Farm Animals, Farm Cottages, Farm-houses, Farming Distribution, Farm Labour, Farmstead, Farm Tools, History of, and Farm Vehicles. Unless you were a Cirencester Agricultural College-type child, this was tedious stuff. The only sen-tence in that volume that caught the eye was the first sentence of 'Rubber': 'When the Spaniards first arrived in Mexico they found the

Indians had waterproof clothes and balls which bounced.'

That is, actually, a brilliant first sentence for an article on rubber: engaging, concise, elegant and convincing. Who wrote it? All 4,030 articles across the twelve volumes are anonymous, so we don't know, but at the beginning of each volume there's a list of its contributors. Many seem to be dons, and most of the ones who aren't are experts with letters after their names. There are far more male contributors than female. In 'Great Lives' there are 13 female contributors out of 112; 'Farming and Fisheries' has 6 female contributors out of a total of 84, and one of them is Lady Hart Dyke of the Lullingstone Silk Farm.

The whole encyclopedia has, to me, the 'voice' of a benign Oxford don explaining something to his or her highly curious and intelligent 12-year-old child. Each article is so thoughtfully and clearly written, with such enthusiasm to impart its knowledge and wisdom in a readable way, that even when you read one on a subject you're not interested in, you imagine the child for whom reading it might have been *the* moment that sparked a lifelong passion, be it for Soil Erosion or the Hotel Industry. Who designed this 'voice'? Whose idea was this whole enterprise?

To find out, I spent an afternoon in the library of the Oxford University Press headquarters, looking through the archive. There's no doubt: the guiding force and guardian of the encyclopedia's 'voice' was a woman called Laura E. Salt, one of its general editors (the other was Geoffrey M. Boumphrey). She had been a schoolteacher and then an HM Inspector for Education. The war years, she explained in one interview in the files, had been 'a splendid time for broiling up ideas as we had no paper for publishing books'. The first edition appeared from 1948 to 1955 and sold well over a million copies.

Miss Salt's method was to divide the volumes into themes – so, for example, you will find 'Japanese' in the 'Mankind' volume; 'Japan' in 'The Universe'; 'Japanese Language' in 'Communications', and 'Japanese Art' in 'The Arts'. Arthur Mee had used a similar method with his ten-volume *Children's Encyclopædia*, which he started in 1908 when the diphthong was still very much in use – and that also had a volume called 'Great Lives'. Mee's encyclopedia went out of print in the early 1960s and the *Oxford Junior Encyclopedia*, aiming at a slightly older age of child, took its place. As Laura Salt wrote, 'Each volume develops a flavour of its own, and encourages the reader to think of knowledge in related wholes rather than in isolated snippets of information.' This is excellent for the vital process of self-education through selective browsing; the only disadvantage is that it made it possible for a non-sciencey child never even to open (or, perhaps, even buy) the 'Industry and Commerce' volume, which had a picture of a power-station on the dust jacket. (That volume, I now discover, has a long article on 'The Tobacco Industry', written in the days before smoking was seen as a bad thing. 'The cut tobacco,' gushes the author, who was probably chain-smoking while writing it, 'known as "rag", is then passed through a heated rotary cylinder which reduces the moisture and brings out the flavour and aroma.')

Laura Salt's other inspired idea was to commission only the very cleverest people in the country to write the articles. The lists of contributors abound with Emeritus Professors and Fellows of the Royal Society. 'Editors', Miss Salt explained, 'found it was far more successful to go to first-class experts, even though these might have little experience of writing for the young. In fact, it is the really great scholar who can see through his or her subject far enough to be able to select the essentials and write simply about them.' That is spot on, especially if you have someone as exacting as Laura Salt to edit each article and make sure every sentence of the sciencey ones is intelligible to a lay person. The result is that the *Oxford Junior Encyclopedia* works well as 'a reference book for all the family', as the reviewer for *The Listener* put it.

But what if you needed to look something up and didn't know which volume to look in? For that, a thirteenth volume, 'Index and Ready Reference', was created. If an index item is in bold type, that means there's a whole article on it; if in roman, it's mentioned but doesn't have a full article. It's fun to look at that index now and see what is and isn't there. There's no mention at all of Mary Seacole, for a start. There's no full article on the Gunpowder Plot, no article on Thomas Cromwell, no mention of Chinese New Year or Diwali, and the index goes from 'Rectum' to 'Red admiral butterfly' without mentioning 'Recycling'. The things they went on about in those days were: Telecommunications, Television Engineering, Dams, Plastics in Industry, Irrigation, Slide Rule, Soil Mechanics and Wireless Telegraphy. New subjects for the 1970s edition included Automation, Computers, Lasers, New Towns, Race Relations and Silicons. The article about computers (in the 'Engineering' volume) comes with the inevitable photograph of a computer the size of a large room with two lab technicians pressing buttons and turning handles.

As well as the strong bias towards male contributors, there's discernible sexism in the prose. 'Man no longer had to live in caves; instead he camped by lakes and marshes . . .' That prehistoric 'he' was to be expected in the 1970s, just as the Roman Empire, and any ship, was 'she'. In any piece on DIY and household repairs, it's 'No one should attempt to repair furniture unless he is certain that he has sufficient skill and knowledge.' For anything about domestic science, it's 'Some modern stoves have special features such as a glass or Perspex oven door to allow the cook to examine what she is cooking.' The 'Home and Health' volume (from which both those examples are taken) is, actually, rather hard-going, with bossy articles on dressmaking divided into numbered sections. 'The straight pieces must be exactly in line with the selvage, and the crosswise pieces on the exact cross.' This is not the kind of thing that any child wants to look up in an encyclopedia, but I suppose it had to be there, for definitiveness's sake. 'Home and Health' was the last volume to be completed, and it shows. Its editor, Winifred Davin, 'complained bitterly' (according to Laura Salt's recollections) 'that her volume was being treated as a waste-paper basket' for unwanted subjects.

But in general, *Oxford Junior Encyclopedia* pieces are the opposite of dull. Their writers believe in the romance of facts. Compare and contrast the gentle breaking of the news (in the *OJE*) that the expression 'cave man' is 'now rather meaningless and misleading', with Wikipedia's instant killing off of the whole romantic concept: 'A caveman is a stock character based upon widespread but anachronistic and conflated concepts of the way in which Neanderthals or early modern humans may have looked and behaved.' *OJE* contributors would never have been as brutal as that; nor would such a heart-sinkingly soulless sentence have been allowed into print by the great Laura Salt – who, the OUP archivist told me, died in 1983 ('her staff obituary does not mention any surviving family').

The *Oxford Junior Encyclopedia* was replaced in the 1990s by the nine-volume *Oxford Children's Encyclopedia*, a different entity entirely. We did buy one for our children but it was never loved. It comes in a blue glossy box and is alphabetical: the volumes go 'Aborigines to Candles', 'Cannibalism to Egypt' and so on. The only nod to the Salt method is that there's still a separate volume called 'Biography' (no longer 'Great Lives'). But the pieces are half the length, so there's no longer any mention of the Faradays moving to rooms over a coach house near Manchester Square when Michael was 5. The abbreviation 'q.v.', ubiquitous in the *OJE*, has been replaced with 'Find out more'. There's no question: it's dumbed down. And, worse, the information has been deromanticized, textbook diagrams replacing those brilliantly chosen photographs. It was reprinted in 2004; but now even that is going to be discontinued, as young people now look everything up online. You just try helping your child to do a project on King John with nothing but the choice between a Wikipedia information torrent and a BBC bitesize article in a jaunty font.

YSENDA MAXTONE GRAHAM is the author of three Slightly Foxed books: *The Real Mrs Miniver, Mr Tibbits's Catholic School* and *Terms & Conditions*.

A Different Kind of Wealth

CHRIS SAUNDERS

As a rather romantic young man in my early twenties, I longed for a
retreat, a cabin by a lake where I could learn to understand nature
and write reams of lapidary poetry. Of course this never came to pass,
not least because I could no more build a habitable hut than I could
fly, but the lure of the self-sustaining rural life remains strong. My
dream might have been inspired by Henry Thoreau's *Walden*, his
account of his life in a hut by a pond which remains an icon of
American literature. In fact it was a book by another, later American
that really inspired me – Robert Francis's *Travelling in Amherst* (1986),
a copy of which I discovered one day in Hay-on-Wye.

I knew, very vaguely, that Francis was a friend of the more famous
Robert, Robert Frost. Very vaguely is how most people now know
Robert Francis. Born in Pennsylvania in 1901, he graduated from
Harvard in 1923 and, determined to live as a poet, built a tiny wooden
house, Fort Juniper, outside Amherst, Massachusetts, and made ends
meet by teaching the violin while trying to persuade magazines to
accept his work. Frost was a near neighbour and mentored Francis,
rather as he had Edward Thomas. As a result, Francis's early collections of poetry, and especially his long domestic epic poem 'Valhalla',
are all rather Frost-like in their depiction of New England nature
and rural life. Later on he found his own voice – playful, relaxed, sly,
concise – and earned some recognition, winning the Academy of

Robert Francis's *Travelling in Amherst: A Poet's Journal, 1930–1950* [in fact the
journal runs from February 1931 to June 1954] (1986) is out of print but we can
try to obtain second-hand copies.

American Poets' award for distinguished lifetime achievement in 1984, three years before
his death. I didn't know any of this at the time
though. I just knew he was a friend of Robert
Frost, who at that point was the biggest star
in my poetic sky.

Now I prefer Francis. Frost had tried farming in New Hampshire, but he soon found
comfort in university departments and lec-
ture tours where his garrulous public persona
earned him a very decent living to support
the writing of his poetry, which became more
cosy and cracker-barrel as he grew older. You can't blame Frost for
making the best of his career, but the purist in me will always cheer
for Francis. He really lived the Thoreauvian life without compromise,
as *Travelling in Amherst*, the diary of his life from 1931 to 1954, shows.

In it Robert Frost makes several appearances, as do Francis's
assorted landladies, his neighbours and many birds, but the focus is
on the author's daily life; the minutiae of existence alongside the joys
and pains of writing for a living. A few of his poems are also included,
showing how he transmuted his observations into verse. (The title of
the book reflects his sense of humour, by the way – he travels no
more than about ten miles during the whole book.) The idea that
home can constitute a universe is very important to Francis, because
for him poetry is an introverted art. As he says in his entry for 22 June
1931: 'The poet is a spider, forever spinning. The novelist is a cater-
pillar, eating great slices of life. But the poet spins his poetry out of
himself, out of next to nothing.'

It is lucky that Francis was comfortable eking substance out of
next to nothing because, as the book makes clear, that is pretty much
what he lived on for twenty years. The diary records the period of his
first modest poetic successes, the building of Fort Juniper, and then
the long drought in the 1940s and '50s when he published almost

nothing. It ends before 1960, when his collection *The Orb Weaver* –
not coincidentally, another spider image – brought him public
recognition. The man's ability to live through failure and poverty
without once diverting from his poetic vocation, and to retain his
good humour, is heroic. It is, in fact, inspirational to read, at what
feels increasingly like the fag end of the consumer era, this entry
from 5 July 1953:

> Though I live far below The American Standard of Living, I am
> not impoverished or pitiful. All bills (except the property tax)
> are paid to date. I own my small home. I am well nourished
> and adequately clothed. Few writers have more propitious con-
> ditions under which to write.

Who needs anything more? To be so utterly beyond material aspir-
ation is surely a joyful state. In fact it seems so thoroughly reasonable
that I forget that Francis's life was singular, based on a willingness to
forgo all kinds of luxury and ease that I am, essentially, too lazy to
give up. Francis had to work hard at his life – he did all his own
repairs, grew his own food, ate a diet of squash, green beans and
tomatoes, and counted his rejection slips. Yet he did it all so whole-
heartedly that, for the brief span of this book at least, his way of life
seems like the only way. It is a very American life, drawing on the
tradition of New England self-reliance that we see in the essays of
Emerson and Thoreau, the creed of owing nothing and creating
everything:

> So far as I know, I am free to go on living here at Fort Juniper
> as long as I go on living. Free to go on with my life. Free to go
> on living.

In middle age I now have reservations about that vision of life.
Self-reliance can so easily become isolation, though it never did for

Francis, whose one luxury was a radio that brought him music and voices from far beyond Amherst. Yet his single-minded life, in which he spun such riches from so little material, is still an inspiration, and this book the one I have reread more than any other. If there were any creed for those of us who feel the need to justify a slightly out-of-the-way life – and as an antiquarian bookseller in a Kindle world, I frequently have to, not least to myself and my bank manager – it would surely be this:

> Every kind of life costs something. The price I pay is different from the price others pay because my life itself is different. I cannot escape payment, but I can make my life worth payment.

CHRIS SAUNDERS has been an antiquarian bookseller at Henry Sotheran since 2004. He is also a freelance writer and the author of two small books on Edward Thomas as well as poems and articles on a variety of bookish subjects. He lives in East Sussex with his wife and daughter in a house that he didn't build himself.

Brief Encounters

HORACE ANNESLEY

'My dear sir,' said Mr James, 'how extremely percipient of you to have identified my person as the author of the – may I say distinct? – volume you eagerly offer, and how pleased I should be to accede to your request were it not that, regrettably, upon leaving Casa Alvisi – that most delightfully hospitable, surely, of all Venetian palazzi? – had I not, as I say, departed this morning without placing in my breast pocket the necessary instrument with which it would in other circumstances have been my pleasure to accede to your so flattering invitation to inscribe, or shall we say to dedicate . . .'

'He means', interrupted the lady at his side, 'that he's forgotten his pen.'

Spencer Somers's copy of *Daisy Miller* was never, alas, inscribed or dedicated, for Edith Wharton didn't have a pen either, and the waiter at Caffè Florian, when summoned, simply had a blunt pencil with which he wrote out a bill for tea and *pandolce*; and eager collector of autographed books though Spencer Somers was, he couldn't bring himself to borrow a waiter's pencil to offer to Henry James.

That encounter took place in 1887, when James and his friend Edith Wharton were staying in Venice with the New York hostess Katherine Bronson (who was later given a bit part in *The Aspern Papers*) and the anecdote comes from Somers's single book, *Tea at*

Spencer Somers, *Tea at Florian's* (1920), is out of print: we regret that we have had difficulty in finding second-hand copies.

Florian's, which was published in 1920. An account of a life deeply devoted to celebrity-chasing, it is both comic and rather pathetic, because though he describes his victims with enthusiasm and a considerable talent for characterization, his encounters with them were almost always unsatisfactory.

The Florian's of the title is of course the celebrated café in the Piazza San Marco in Venice, where Somers lay in wait for his victims on the (perfectly accurate) theory that sooner or later anyone who was anyone would at some time sit down in the Sala Greca or the Sala Orientale or at one of the outside tables for afternoon tea. He became well known to the waiters there: if he seemed to have nothing better to do in the afternoons than sit over a cup of Darjeeling or Gunpowder Supreme, it was because he didn't have anything better to do.

Somers was born in Tunbridge Wells in 1850, the son of Admiral the Honourable Aubrey Somers, KCMG. The Admiral was a singular figure in the Navy of his time. Like so many seamen, he was a prolific knitter and, as Somers records,

created something of a legend by sitting knitting Balaclavas with his First Lieutenant on the bridge of his warship HMS *Respite* during a skirmish arising in 1855 from the Anglo-French siege of Petropavlosk-Kamchatsky, and being heard at one point to cry: 'No, purl *two*, knit *three* Hardy, you bloody fool. Now, hard a-port and fire at will.'

Spencer, the Admiral's only son, was educated at home by a series of governesses (he went to Uppingham, but only for one week), and at the age of 19 inherited a large family fortune from his aunt, Lady Felicia Somers, the familiar advocate of comprehensive abstinence, and so was able to devote his life to his two passions: Venice, and collecting signed or inscribed copies of books by authors visiting that city. He became a familiar figure among the English residents: unusually tall (he was well over six feet), he was extremely thin and almost invariably wore black, so that on dark nights passers-by not infrequently knocked him into the canal near his apartment at 30 via Marcantonio Bragadin (once occupied by Lord Byron). Fortunately his height was such that he was able to walk to the nearest steps with his head above water, and at worst only suffered the latest of a series of severe colds.

He became an almost lethal collector of signed editions, but encounters with their authors were rarely smooth (he was once knocked down by Baron Corvo after unwisely asking him whether he was 'anyone in particular'). In 1881 he was delighted to see two of the most celebrated contemporary poets sitting together at Florian's. Browning and Tennyson were playing cribbage: on losing a point one had accurately to quote a line from the works of the other. Tennyson (wrote Somers)

> was winning easily, quoting to Browning lines purporting to come from the latter's poem *Sordello*. Since he had largely forgotten this early and extravagantly obscure poem, Browning was unable to contest Tennyson's quotations, and as I approached finally lost his temper, and knocking over his glass of Burton's Pale Ale (especially imported for him by Florian's) he stumped off across the piazza, scowling. This put Tennyson in an excellent humour, and when I got home I found he had not merely signed his name to my copy of his complete poems, but had added the legend: 'Who's Browning, anyway? – A.T.'

Tea at Florian's is full of such unexpected glimpses of the authors of Somers's time. One of the most interesting encounters occurred in 1900 when, recognizing Marcel Proust taking tea with his friend the composer Reynaldo Hahn, he rushed back to his apartment to fetch his copy of *Les Plaisirs et les jours*:

> Proust and his friend were beautifully dressed in matching suits of grey silk with identical cravats of heliotrope and with twin

mauve *mouchoirs* tucked into their breast pockets. They were in deep conversation, so I stood silently beside them for some time before, lightly touching Proust on the shoulder, I remarked: *'Bonjour, M. Proust – Mais ou sont les neiges d'antan?'* He immediately leapt to his feet with a cry of *'Foutre le camp!'* (a remark I later found to have an obscene connotation). I retired. Later that week I read in *La Nuova Venezia* that Proust had been arrested for brawling in the street with two gondoliers and a *poliziotto*; the great author was subsequently known in Venice as *Pugile* or 'Bruiser' Proust.

Somers's private library was, sadly, dispersed after his death, and such treasures as his copy of *Ziska: The Problem of a Wicked Soul*, signed by its author, Marie Corelli, and the autograph of 'Gunga Din' written out on the back of a Florian menu by Rudyard Kipling, have vanished. *Tea at Florian's* does however contain several portraits he took with his 1888 Eastman Kodak camera, including a rare photograph of W. S. Gilbert and Sir Arthur Sullivan in gondoliers' costume, arm-in-arm with Mrs Corelli and Giovanni, the gondolier she later took to Stratford to row the gondola she kept on the Avon. They appear to be singing. The illustrations also reveal a few figures clearly unrecognized by Somers: one, for instance, of the façade of San Zaccaria, shows a somewhat large and ungainly man dressed in what appear to be velvet knickerbockers with, on his arm, a younger man in white duck trousers and a shirt open to the navel. They are clearly Oscar Wilde and 'Bosie' Douglas, on holiday in February 1895 after the success of *The Importance of Being Earnest*. Another shows the Piazza and Florian's under the *acqua alta* or flood of 1908. In his text, Somers tells us that on the day before the flood, when it was anticipated but not positively forecast, he had called at the Calle Sangallo, on a corner overlooking the Grand Canal, to meet a writer who had recently had a success with his third novel, *A Room with a View*:

Mr Edward Forster's novel *Where Angels Fear to Tread* had a great effect upon me, showing him to be, as I was, a lover of Italy; and hearing that he was in Venice I went immediately to the Librario Marco Polo and purchased his latest book, *A Room with a View*. Sure enough, on the following morning he was seated at Florian's, well away from the rain, with a companion dressed in the uniform of the British police force. He seemed moderately pleased to accede to my request for his autograph, and more reluctantly to sit for his photograph. However, a friend who was accompanying him struck in with 'Eddie, you can't be photographed in that old jacket. What would your mother say?' This rather authoritarian rebuke resulted in Mr Forster agreeing to return to Florian's on the following afternoon at the same hour, when I might take his picture.

Alas, during the night the water rose, flooding the piazza and surrounding streets, and parts of Chioggia. I stood on a piece of high pavement opposite Florian's. The boards were of course up, and the caffè closed. I took a photograph of the scene. Only, some days later, when the photographic firm delivered the prints of my pictures, did I see, outside the caffè, the melancholy figure of Edward Morgan Forster, dressed in impeccable tweeds, the water just above his knees. I have always viewed this as a tribute not only to the courteous nature of the author, but the very nature of the English Gentleman.

Somers died in his Venice rooms in the autumn of 1920. He was found sitting at his desk, a pen in his hand, and at his side a small pile of the recently published *Tea at Florian's*, which he was about to inscribe. Somehow, it seems an apt way for him to have gone.

HORACE ANNESLEY used to work for the North Eastern Gas Board. His hobbies are writing and collecting autographs of important contemporary figures, of which he has a large number.

Chalet Girls

DAISY HAY

In the summer of 1994 I took my family on a literary pilgrimage to the town of Pertisau am Achensee in the Austrian Tyrol. We were on our way to the wedding of family friends in Hungary, and the detour to Pertisau entailed hours of additional driving on the part of my father. Lesser parents might have refused to spend a day and a half of a packed holiday acceding to the whims of a 13-year-old. I, however, was the possessor of an endlessly kind and patient father, and a mother who was quietly almost as keen on visiting Pertisau as I was.

Pertisau doesn't feature on most Tyrolean itineraries, but every year it nevertheless receives a trickle of English visitors. These visitors – mostly women – all head to the deserted Alpenhof Hotel, and it was there my parents took the photograph I'm looking at now, of me holding a copy of *The School at the Chalet* by Elinor M. Brent-Dyer.

Elinor M. Brent-Dyer was a teacher from South Shields who visited Pertisau in the early 1920s. The first of her school stories set at the Alpenhof Hotel, which she transformed into the setting for her Chalet School, was published in 1925. Fifty-eight Chalet books followed, the last appearing

---

A complete list of Elinor M. Brent-Dyer's Chalet School books can be obtained from Friends of the Chalet School at The Vicarage, Church Street, Coleford, Radstock BA3 5NG or on their website www.chaletschool.org.uk.

posthumously in 1970. The books have been continuously in print ever since. Today you can become a Friend of the Chalet School or join the New Chalet Club; or, if you prefer your fandom in virtual form, you can join in lively and daily-updated debates about the books on the online Chalet School Bulletin Board. At the precise moment that I'm writing this, the Chalet School Bulletin Board tells me that it has 1,452 registered members, 21 of whom are online and in discussion about the series as I type.

In my teens I was a paid-up junior member of the Friends of the Chalet School, although my courage always failed me when it came to attending social Chalet School gatherings. Looking back I'm not sure I really wanted to meet other devotees, so vivid was my relationship with the books. The Chalet School was my solitary pleasure and its orderly systems offered a refuge from the emotional chaos of adolescence. I can't quite remember what I thought as I stood outside the Alpenhof Hotel, and looking at photographs of it now I wonder whether I was disappointed in its dilapidated grandeur. This summer I've been rereading the Chalet School books to try to understand why I dragged my father and my cross 9-year-old sister to look at an empty building in a sleepy lakeside town, and why my mother connived with me in the dragging. I haven't reread all fifty-nine books, but I have dipped in and out in roughly chronological order, alighting on old favourites as well as those titles of which I have no memory. I've had, I will freely admit, the most glorious time in the process.

The Chalet School story, in very brief form, goes like this. In the first book Madge Bettany opens a school in the Tyrol, in conjunction with her French business partner, Mademoiselle LePattre. They have three pupils to begin with: Madge's much younger sister Joey, Mademoiselle LePattre's young cousin Simone, and Grizel Cochrane, a friend of Joey's. From these beginnings the school grows in size and strength until it is forced by the Anschluss to close. It reopens again first on Guernsey, then in Herefordshire, then on a small island off the Welsh coast, before finally settling in Switzerland, where the final third of the books are set. As the school matures, so do its founding members. Madge Bettany marries a doctor early in the series and retires from active running of the school, although Brent-Dyer is at pains to remind readers that Madge remains chair of its board throughout its existence. Marriage to doctors is a recurring theme, courtesy of Madge's husband Jem establishing a sanatorium near the school and thus ensuring graduating girls a ready supply of eligible medics.

Madge's younger sister Joey, meanwhile, becomes the beating heart of the series, present in virtually every book. Joey starts life as an imaginative and naughty schoolgirl, a vividly realized creation who is always in the thick of things. After she leaves school she marries a doctor of her own, becomes a bestselling author and defies the laws of gynaecology to produce triplets, two sets of twins and assorted other singly born children. At the end of the series her offspring number eleven and she is to be found threatening to inflict quads on her long-suffering husband and elder daughters. Other girls, meanwhile, fill her place as leaders in the school. Notable among the second and third generations of Chalet girls are Mary-Lou Trelawney (who begins school life as a fairly normal human being and ends it as a paragon of monstrous competence) and Joey's eldest daughter Len, a much put-upon creature who has all of her mother's sense of responsibility and none of her redeeming qualities.

As this summary perhaps indicates, there is much about the Chalet School which is deeply weird. This is particularly true of the later books, which lose the carefree happiness of the stories set in the Tyrol. The girls in the Swiss books march everywhere in lines; every minute of their days is filled with ruthless efficiency. Packs of prefects stride up and down the main stairs like anxious dictators, stamping out spontaneity wherever it threatens. Hapless temporary members of staff who don't conform to the school's values are promptly sacked: in one case a promising career is almost derailed because an inexperienced new teacher fails to appreciate the marvels of Mary-Lou.

Oddest of all perhaps is the treatment of the 'Middles', girls in their early to mid teens who are consistently characterized as delin-quents in terms more suited to the inhabitants of a zoo than a school. The school is also a thoroughly dangerous place to be. Not a term passes without someone almost falling off a mountain precipice or into a lake, or becoming dangerously ill. Towards the end of the series, when Brent-Dyer herself was ill and some of the writing was done by others, the litany of near tragedies becomes parodic. You can't help feeling that any sensible parent would have removed their daughter from such a perilous institution within a term.

And yet. It is easy to be rude about the Chalet School: the very repetitiveness of the series makes it endlessly mockable. But the oddness alone, entertaining though it is, doesn't explain the books' enduring appeal. Its magic is elusive but it is there, apparent even on an adult rereading. Part of it lies in Brent-Dyer's attention to detail: interiors and food are lovingly and realistically evoked. Her world runs with the precision of a Swiss clock, and it becomes entirely possible to sink unquestioningly into its exotic foreignness. I know the German names for meals and how to work the 24-hour clock thanks to the Chalet School girls' baffling insistence on having their *kaffee und kuchen* at sixteen o'clock. I also never doubted the peda-gogical logic of speaking a different language every day, or paused to wonder how the school's proud trilingualism worked in practice.

More seriously though, Brent-Dyer doesn't shy away from dealing with difficult subjects. The girls of whom she approves are for the most part fairly appalling individuals, but those whom she writes as difficult are much more interesting. Grizel Cochrane is one, the vic-tim of a neglected childhood who is made bitter by a lonely middle age. Grizel eventually finds happiness (with a doctor, of course), but only after her deep depression has been thoughtfully drawn. Joey's 'bad' daughter Margot is equally intriguing: dismissed as hot-tempered and unmanageable throughout her childhood (and in a manner at odds with Brent-Dyer's insistence on the perfection of Joey's parenting), Margot grows up into an independent-minded person who turns her back on her family at the end of the series in rather spectacular fashion.

Brent-Dyer is particularly interested in girls who are parentless or alone, and she is unsparing in her depiction of the sometimes downright abusive upbringings that throw them on the mercy of others. Such girls become completely enveloped in the embrace of the school, which is notable at all stages for its capacious and generous understanding of family. There are moments of real grief in the series but the books are rarely sentimental. The death of Jacynth Hardy's aunt in *Gay Lambert at the Chalet School* made me cry when I first read it, and it made me cry again this summer.

The series also contains one truly great book. *The Chalet School in Exile* tells the story of the school's forced closure in 1938. Published in 1940, it relates how Joey and a group of pupils and staff are forced to flee Austria on foot after they defend an elderly Jew from the violence of the mob. In a chapter called 'A Nazi Sport' Brent-Dyer reveals the faces of the crowd, young Austrian men infected with the ideals of their invaders. Throughout she emphasizes the distinction between Nazis and civilians, and her wartime school story presents Austrian and German citizens with great humanity. The priest who helps the girls to escape and is murdered as a result; the schoolgirl called home to work in a Nazi munitions factory; idealistic young men forced to fly planes for a regime they hate: these characters and others lift *The Chalet School in Exile* far above the realms of an ordinary school story and they do so in a book published less than a year after the start of the war. Most striking of all is the tale of Herr Marini, who refuses to remove his daughter Maria from the school and who vanishes into a concentration camp as a result of his disobedience. Brent-Dyer reserves the merciful news of Herr Marini's death until the end of the book, carefully tracking his daughter's progression from carefree schoolgirl to haunted young woman in and out of the depiction of larger political dramas. There is no falsely happy ending here. The only hope offered at the end of *Exile* is that the values inculcated by the Chalet School will ultimately prevail in a war-torn world.

During my summer of rereading, it has been those values that have struck me most deeply. I'm not talking here about the jolly-hockey-sticks stuff on fair play and joining in, or about the religiosity displayed by Brent-Dyer's favourite characters. Much more interesting, in these turbulent times, is that the school is a model of European integration, and it stays true to the importance of being part of a community of nations even when that community is ripped apart by war. Brent-Dyer may have taken my family to Pertisau in 1994 but she also left a longer-lasting impression, making me, aged 13, an ardent believer in the European project. For that, and for much else besides, I will always remain a Chalet School fan.

DAISY HAY is the author of *Young Romantics* and *Mr and Mrs Disraeli*. She still goes on literary pilgrimages but sadly these no longer involve school stories.

Harvey Learns the Ropes

ANDREW JOYNES

I have been aware of the themes of Rudyard Kipling's novel *Captains Courageous* (1897) almost all my life. I was given the book by my father when I was a child, just after the family emigrated to Canada in what turned out to be a failed attempt to escape the privations of post-war Britain, where daily life was governed by the ration card. After the transatlantic liner docked in Quebec in 1951, we walked up to the city heights to have breakfast in a diner. As he began to eat, my father said, 'These are the first pork sausages I have tasted since 1940 . . .'

Two days previously, when my brother and I were about to climb into bunks in the family cabin, we had been told by a passing steward that the ship would be crossing Newfoundland's Grand Banks during the night. He spoke of the days when codfish were so numerous in these warm shallow seas that they slowed the onward passage of sailing ships through the ocean. But by the time we woke the next day and rushed to the rail to see this wonder of nature, the ship had left Newfoundland far behind and was about to enter the St Lawrence. On both rocky shores of the vast river mouth, pine trees crowded down to the water's edge. Ocean spray breaking on forest: this was my childhood image of an immense New World, with my father's delight in his arrival breakfast a hint of the abundant life to come.

When he gave *Captains Courageous* to me, my father described the opening episode of the book: a teenage boy falls overboard from a transatlantic liner at night and is hauled into a dory by a deckhand

---

Rudyard Kipling's *Captains Courageous* (1897) is available in various print-on-demand editions. We can also obtain good second-hand copies.

from a Grand Banks fishing schooner. Unsurprisingly, the story resonated with me immediately, for to the child's mind the story of *Captains Courageous* is one of rescue. A boy falls into the sea, has adventures and forms friendships, and in due course is returned to his grieving parents.

To the adult mind, however, the story is one of redemption. Harvey Cheyne Jr is the spoilt son of an American railway magnate, and he slips through the rails after swooning from the effects of a head-dizzying cigar which he has lit to show off to the card-players in the liner's smoking-room. The agent of his redemption is Disko Troop, master and owner of the schooner *We're Here*, who tells the arrogant boy that there can be no question of taking him back to port before they have caught enough fish to cover the costs of the schooner's voyage (it is now May, and the schooner will not have its hold full of salt cod until at least September).

Harvey insists his father will pay, but Disko cannot believe that anyone, even a railway magnate, could be rich enough to reimburse him for an abandoned voyage. When Harvey loses his temper and accuses the schooner's crew of stealing his money, Disko responds with a clip round the ear that brings Harvey to his senses, and by the end of the first chapter Kipling has tidily set the scene for the boy's remarkable character transformation during a busy summer at sea.

As with all sea stories, the reader of *Captains Courageous* becomes a kind of stowaway, an eavesdropping presence in the little floating world of the *We're Here*. Conversations are overheard, characters are recognized, tensions noted. Kipling soon establishes the personalities that are key to his central story of Harvey's transformation from braggart into self-reliant stalwart. Principal among them are Disko, the stern but kindly captain, and his son Dan Troop, a boy of Harvey's age with whom the newcomer forms a close friendship.

The other crew members provide the chorus to this story. They literally teach Harvey the ropes, taking him on a daily circuit of the schooner's deck and requiring him to lay his hand on each piece of rigging as its arcane name is called out, reinforcing the catechism with a rope's end if he makes a mistake. The black cook, who speaks only Gaelic, is human flotsam from the tides of Empire in the North Atlantic: he comes from Nova Scotia, where the descendants of runaway slaves who waged a successful guerrilla war against the British army in Jamaica were resettled at the end of the eighteenth century. Gifted with second sight, he observes with silent and mystic approval Harvey's transformation.

Throughout his writings, Kipling finds grace in everyday trades. There is a remarkable passage in *Captains Courageous* where he describes in detail the process of dressing and salting the cod which have been brought back to the schooner by the dories (these are then stacked inside each other on the schooner's deck like teacups on a kitchen dresser). It is almost as though he considers his own writer's craft to be inferior to manual skill and dexterity, and he leaves the reader in no doubt that, in acquiring such journeyman skills, Harvey's moral redemption has begun: 'At the end of an hour, Harvey would have given the world to rest; for fresh, wet cod weigh more than you would think, and his back ached with the steady pitching. But he felt for the first time in his life that he was one of a working gang of men, took pride in the thought, and held on sullenly . . .'

When Kipling was writing this book over a century ago, there was still an abundance of fish on the Grand Banks. From medieval times onwards, salt cod had been a staple of the European diet: the *bacalão* that one finds in Mediterranean markets today takes its name from Baccalieu, a Newfoundland fishing-ground. But such abundance could only be maintained by traditional fishing methods such as those described in *Captains Courageous*, where wily skippers like Disko Troop would study the weather and the sky and the movement of birds and whales and bait-fish to indicate the whereabouts of the cod, and then send his crew out in dories to catch them with baited lines. In modern times these teeming waters were rendered barren by international fishing fleets, whose crews used sonar indicators to find the fish and then scooped them into wide-mouthed, close-meshed seine nets that scraped the very silt from the seabed. A quarter of a century ago the Grand Banks were closed to all fishing by the Canadian government (although today there are hopes that the cod are returning and that a limited amount of sustainable fishing might be permitted).

With such a profound sense of environmental loss there has to be an elegiac quality to the reading of *Captains Courageous* today – as indeed there was to a radio programme I made about the Grand Banks some years ago, when I travelled to Newfoundland and to Gloucester, Massachusetts, the home port in Kipling's day of hundreds of fishing schooners like the *We're Here*. An old lady I met there said to me, 'Can you imagine it? "No Fishing" signs on the Grand Banks! That's like putting "No Farming" signs on the American prairies . . .'

Kipling wrote *Captains Courageous* in New England, where he spent half a decade in the early 1890s. He had gone there after marrying Carrie Balestier, a girl from Vermont. These were intensely productive years, during which he wrote *The Jungle Book* and its sequel, published a collection of short stories called *The Day's Work*, and gathered some of his most popular poems into the verse collection *Barrack-room Ballads*. But it was the novel subtitled 'A Story of the Grand Banks' that expressed his sense of the immense potential of the great continent where he had settled.

Nowhere is Kipling's sense of North America's industrial and entrepreneurial potential more dramatically expressed than in the dénouement of *Captains Courageous*. The *We're Here* is the first schooner in the Grand Banks fleet to fill her hold with cod, and Disko Troop speedily sails her back to Gloucester to name a 'take it or leave it' price to the town's fish merchants, who are avid for the new season's catch. Harvey sends a telegram to his parents, who have been in California all summer, grieving for the son they believed lost in the spring, and the news of his survival strikes like a thunderbolt. In a remarkable modernist sequence, which evokes the hissing of steam trains and the pounding of pistons, Harvey Cheyne Sr enlists the help of his fellow railway magnates to make a crossing of the North American continent in record time. He and his wife arrive in Gloucester to see their transformed son play a confident part in the tally of the schooner's cargo, and in due course he and Disko Troop plan a joint future for their two sons which mysteriously corresponds to the black cook's second-sight predictions.

When he wrote *Captains Courageous*, Kipling may well have been intending to stay permanently in New England, but by the time the book was published a bitter quarrel with his brother-in-law had led him and his wife to return to England. My own family's New World idyll ended in the mid-1950s, with my father waving bleakly to his departing wife and sons from the same Quebec dockside where the family had disembarked four years before.

Perhaps because of those defining childhood sea journeys, I have always loved model boats and ships, and in recent years I have built a number of them. During my visit to Gloucester, I went to a ship-building museum and bought some plans of old Grand Banks schooners. Not many of these beautiful vessels have survived, because most were built of pine, which is prone to rot and decay. The plans show the lovely lines of the typical Gloucester schooner: a long hull, a foremast shorter than the mainmast, and a fore-and-aft sail plan which means the vessel can sail close to the wind. I built a display model showing a schooner under full sail, with three little carved boxwood figures in the stern. One is crouched at the wheel, with his legs flexed like a weightlifter. Another is seated by the rail, out of the wind, his arms clasping his knees. And the third is reclining on the hatch-cover, hands behind his head. Disko, Harvey and Dan, the central figures in Kipling's tale of fatherhood and redemption. If, like a painting, a model could be given a title, I would call it *Heading Home*.

ANDREW JOYNES worked as a BBC producer and is now a writer and historian. He is the author of *Medieval Ghost Stories: An Anthology of Miracles, Marvels and Prodigies* and *Tracking the Major: Sketches from the Powell-Cotton Museum.*

Lives and Letters

MICHAEL HOLROYD

No one asked me to be a biographer. Quite the opposite. My grand-father hoped I might set off for India and make a career at the tea plantations there. He had been presented with some shares in one of the Assam tea companies by his father. He used these shares as if they were tickets that took him on a summer holiday which he called 'following the business'. What he really wanted was to go abroad without his family from time to time. I saw a photo of him in India once: he was smiling in a way I had never seen him smile at home. And he was encircled by rather bemused-looking planters.

Back at home he taught me the skills of making a proper cup of tea. It was not easy: how to hold the cup correctly; how to boil the water to an exact temperature – and then how to engage the small spoons of tea with water at the right moment. Then there was the difficulty of preparing the milk and adding it. Sugar was never toler-ated. Writing a biography was far easier than preparing a correct cup of tea – or so it seemed to me. In the end I wrote a small biography of my grandfather and placed it in my autobiography.

Most people do not encourage members of their family to become biographers. There is no telling what trouble they will get into. If you write fiction any member of your family who appears on the pages of your book can be hidden by a different name that prevents them being recognized. But biographers are always invading other people's families uninvited, writing about the dead who cannot answer them and presenting what they have written to their subjects' families and friends. It's no surprise we are not welcome.

I was fortunate in never being at a university, going instead to the public library for my education. In the library I found hundreds of possible subjects lined up in alphabetical order and waiting to be chosen. There they all were: Dickens, Samuel Johnson, Hugh Kingsmill, Shakespeare. Which one would you have chosen? I chose Hugh Kingsmill. He seemed to have something the others didn't have: an absence of biographies about him (though he wrote some biographies himself – all of them safely out of print). He was, I thought, an obvious choice.

I finished my biography of him within two years – keeping alive by doing odd jobs and writing reviews of other people's biographies. Over the next two years I sent my typescript to sixteen publishers who sent it back to me with a polite letter. They thanked me for sending it to them and implied that they would have very much liked to publish it: but unfortunately couldn't. They were sorry – and so was I. Sorrow filled the air. But eventually it was taken by someone who had recently given up publishing: Martin Secker. He was, someone told me by way of explanation, almost blind. Mine was the last

Caroline Forbes

book he published in his life and he did so with a colleague. It was brought out in 1964 by the Unicorn Press and I was given a generous advance of £25. This came in useful when Kingsmill's second wife objected to a couple of pages in which she appeared and I paid for the rewriting. This rare first edition revealed that it was 'the strange and mysterious quality of her silences which exerted so compelling a power'. I wish she had been more silent with me.

I was gradually learning the complexities of biography which was almost as difficult as my grandfather's tea-making. My father, if asked, would say that I was a historian, which sounded more respectable. He could not see how I would make a career from writing and wished I had become a scientist. If I had a proper career I could, he said, write people's Lives on Sundays – and, if absolutely necessary, on Saturdays too. What more could I need?

As it was, one of the publishers who had amiably turned down my Kingsmill suggested I should try someone else – preferably someone not unknown but not yet written about. Such subjects are hard to find, I discovered, but eventually I came up with Lytton Strachey. He was a biographer without a biography. What could be better? Indeed he was so good a choice that I was given twice the £25 advance for my first biography. But since it took me seven years to complete the book I had to renegotiate this part of my contract as many times as Britain negotiated joining – and then leaving – Europe.

In one of his essays the Bloomsbury art critic Clive Bell had written after Strachey's death in 1932 that it would be impossible to write his biography for a long time. It certainly took me a long time to write his Life – though that was not what Bell had in mind. In the early 1960s homosexuality was still illegal. It was brave of some of Strachey's friends to talk to me about this. 'Shall I be put in jail?' one of them asked. 'Will I be allowed to watch cricket any more at Lord's?' asked another. It seems ridiculous now, and it was fortunate that the law changed shortly before my biography was published in 1967. Some of the most charming readers of the book were men who invited me to dinner – but were disappointed.

What involved me most deeply was Strachey's extraordinary relationship with Dora Carrington. Though my biographies usually have a man's name on the title page, women take over many chapters. This was inevitably true with my next subject, the artist Augustus John. Walking along the streets of Chelsea in London he sometimes patted the heads of children in case, he explained, 'they are some of mine'.

. Sometimes I'm asked how I choose the people whose biographies I write. And I have no idea – no memory of choosing any of them. The fact is, as it were, they choose me, or to put it another way, a minor character in one book gets my attention and becomes my next subject. When I began writing about Ellen Terry (having got to know her when working on my Life of Bernard Shaw), I had no intention of writing about her fellow-actor on the stage Henry Irving – but it was impossible to leave him out. And not leaving him out opened the door to both his and her children. So what had begun as a single short pen-portrait of one person expanded into a group biography covering two generations over a period of a century. No one was more surprised than me.

Am I writing a biography now? Certainly not! Or rather I don't think so. But of course anything may happen on the next page.

MICHAEL HOLROYD has been studying his 'Ancestors in the Attic', which is the title he has given to an illustrated book he is struggling to prepare.

Coming attractions

SUE GAISFORD is gripped by the Asquiths' wartime letters · MICHAEL LEAPMAN stands up (and sits down) for George Bernard Shaw · AMANDA THEUNISSEN follows Kim to India · ANTHONY GARDNER finds his way through Celtic mists · LAURA FREEMAN discovers the tragedy behind the work of A. A. Milne · PETER PARKER enjoys a taste of life in Victorian Shoreditch · ANN KENNEDY SMITH meets E. M. Forster's great-aunt · ARIANE BANKES explores Trieste with Jan Morris

Bibliography

A. L. Barker, *Innocents*; *The Joy-Ride and After*; *The Middling*;
  Life Stories   35

Elinor M. Brent-Dyer, The Chalet School books   80

Emily Brontë, *Wuthering Heights*   47

The Dragon Book of Verse   41

Robert Francis, *Travelling in Amherst: A Poet's Journal*   71

Michael Holroyd: on writing biography   91

Erich Kästner, *When I Was a Little Boy*   13

Rudyard Kipling, *Captains Courageous*   86

Gavin Lyall, *The Wrong Side of the Sky*; *The Most Dangerous Game*;
  Midnight Plus One; *Shooting Script*; *Judas Country*   30

Maurice Maeterlinck, *The Life of the Bee*   25

Vivien Noakes, *Edward Lear: The Life of a Wanderer*   7

George Orwell, *Essays*   58

The *Oxford Junior Encyclopedia*   65

Marcel Proust, *Remembrance of Things Past*   18

Frank Reynolds, the *Punch* cartoons of   53

Spencer Somers, *Tea at Florian's*   75

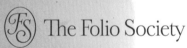